PRAGUE

PRAGUE

Christine Adams

Photographs by Mark Smith

Tauris Parke Books, London

The author would like to thank Caroline Davidson, Věra-Blanka Kymličková, Jiři Musil and Pete de Bolla for their help in the production of this book.

Published by Tauris Parke Books
110 Gloucester Avenue
London NW1 8JA
In association with KEA Publishing Services Ltd, London

TRAVEL TO LANDMARKS
Series Editor: Judy Spours
Editorial Assistant: Elizabeth Harcourt
Designers: Holdsworth Associates
Maps by Charles C. Adams
All photographs by Mark Smith, except pages 26 and 112.

The Cataloguing in Publication Date for this book is available from the British Library, London.

ISBN 1-85043 312-7

Photosetting by Litho Link Ltd, Welshpool, Powys, UK
Colour separation by Fabbri, Milan, Italy
Printed by Fabbri, Milan, Italy

Frontispiece The buildings around the Old Town Square reveal the rich architectural history of Prague: behind their Early Baroque façades these houses have preserved many Romanesque and Gothic features. The square itself was originally a market place. It was the heart of the town founded in 1230 on the right bank of the Vltava and is the centre of historic Prague.

Contents

Introduction

Four former royal towns make up the historic centre of Prague: Hradčany, the Lesser Quarter, the Old Town and the New Town. They were founded in the thirteenth and fourteenth centuries on the banks of the Vltava and share an architectural heritage of remarkable beauty and diversity. Though the towns were united under a single municipal government in the eighteenth century, their different traditions are still apparent to the visitor today. The left bank was settled by the aristocracy, eager to live near the Castle on the Hradčany headland. They built their palaces and churches in the town of Hradčany at the Castle gates or lower down the hill in the Lesser Quarter. The hilltops of the left bank overlook the flat expanse of the Old Town where groups of merchants built their villages near the river. Rapid growth of the town led to the foundation of the last royal town in 1348, the New Town, which carried on the mercantile and craft traditions of the Old.

The four separate communities were brought together during the coronation ceremonies of the kings and queens of Bohemia. The procession to the Castle wound its way through the towns, involving the citizens in the pageantry and pomp of the event. Visitors to the city today are encouraged to follow part of the route taken by the procession. The Royal Way begins at the Powder Tower, on the site of former fortifications between the Old Town and the New Town, and leads up to the Castle. Along the way there are any number of sights to admire: Baroque and Rococo palaces and statues, Gothic towers, decorative Renaissance façades; the Old Town Square, the Charles Bridge leading from the Old Town to the Lesser Quarter, which is dominated by the dome and tower of St Nicholas Church. The differences between the towns become apparent as the route leads from the modern centre of Prague in the New Town past the wide range of styles in the Old Town and the Baroque of the Lesser Quarter up the hill to the splendours of Hradčany and the Castle itself, dominating the skyline by day and night, when its floodlit buildings maintain their watch over the city.

The Royal Way is a colourful introduction to Prague. It implies, however, stability and continuity that have in fact been very rare in the history of the city. Apart from the Přemyslids, who ruled the kingdom of Bohemia from the ninth century until 1306, George of Poděbrady (1458–71) was the only Czech king of Bohemia. Otherwise the

The medieval Charles Bridge connects the Old Town and the Lesser Quarter. With its Baroque 'avenue of statues', it is a striking example of the combinations of styles in the four royal towns that make up the historic centre of Prague. The theme is taken up again in the view of the Lesser Quarter Church of St Nicholas – a High Baroque masterpiece – through the Lesser Quarter bridge towers, dating from the twelfth and fifteenth centuries.

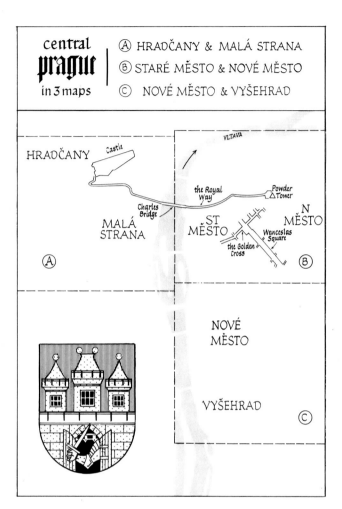

central **prague** in 3 maps

Ⓐ HRADČANY & MALÁ STRANA
Ⓑ STARÉ MĚSTO & NOVÉ MĚSTO
Ⓒ NOVÉ MĚSTO & VYŠEHRAD

HRADČANY

Castle

VLTAVA

the Royal Way

Charles Bridge

Powder Tower

MALÁ STRANA

ST MĚSTO

N MĚSTO

Wenceslas Square

the Golden Cross

Ⓐ

Ⓑ

NOVÉ MĚSTO

VYŠEHRAD

Ⓒ

Right The Castle on Hradčany Hill dominates Prague. Building began under the Přemyslid dynasty that ruled Bohemia from the ninth century until 1326. Over the centuries, this fortress and palace, seat of religious and state power, evolved into a town within a town, clustered around three courtyards and extending into the gardens outside the fortifications.

Overleaf Looking down on to the Old Town Square from the tower of the Old Town hall.

kingdom was ruled by a succession of foreign dynasties such as the French Luxemburgs in the fourteenth century, the Polish Jagiellos after 1471 and the Habsburgs, who ruled from 1526 until the collapse of the Austro-Hungarian Empire in 1918. When they turned their attention to Prague, these rulers all brought outside influences to bear on the royal towns and involved French, German and Italian architects in ambitious building programmes emulated by the nobility. Not only the monarchy was imported: the dynamism of Prague was in part the result of the large numbers of foreign settlers. Czechs, Germans and Jews all participated in shaping the city.

These developments brought Bohemia into the mainstream of European history. They also involved the kingdom in a number of European wars and generated domestic conflicts opposing Germans, Jews and Czechs; burghers, aristocrats and Crown and, from the fifteenth century, Hussite Protestants and Catholic Habsburgs. The Habsburg victory at the Battle of White Mountain in 1620 had a determining effect on the culture and history of the city through the expropriation and exile of the Protestants. In the light of the civil strife and continental wars in which Prague became embroiled, it is remarkable that so much of its past is still visible today – having survived even the depredations of the Nazi occupation and the Second World War.

Until the Velvet Revolution of November 1989 that ousted the Communist government in power since 1948, Czechoslovakia was generally associated in the West with its abandonment by its allies in 1938, the Soviet tanks that crushed the Prague Spring of 1968 or the surreal absurdities of life under the post-1968 regime. It is only recently that what is now the Czech and Slovak Republic emerged from beneath the ice and behind the Iron Curtain. Prague is a very inviting prospect for those who have redrawn their maps of Europe. This book is an introduction to the historic royal towns that are so evocative of the ambitions and clashes of burghers, nobility, Church and Crown. Taking each one of them in turn, it closely relates history and architecture, making the buildings central to an account of the events and people who shaped them and considering important patrons and buildings in some detail. The Castle, palaces, churches and streets of the four towns have many stories to tell; tales which make visiting them all the more interesting.

1   Hradčany

Entering Prague, as we did by the Carlsbad road, you do not see the city until you have fairly passed through its gate; but when, crossing the Loretanska Platz, your carriage is stopped on the terrace of the Hradshin to have the wheels locked, for the frightfully precipitous descent to the bridge, you have such a view presented to your eyes as fully justifies the appellation bestowed on this most beautiful 'Praha', by one of her own most loving sons – 'Fair City of the Hundred Towers' – and such indeed she is.

Travels in Bohemia, by an Old Traveller (London, 1857)

This place is firmly protected on the north side by the deep gorge of the stream Brusnice but on the south side a broad mountain with many rocks which is called Petřín rises above its surroundings. The mountain bends in the manner of the dolphin, the sea pig, towards the river.

The Chronicle of Bohemia, Cosmas (*c.*1122)

The Castle

Legend has it that it was Princess Libuše, founder of the Přemyslid dynasty, who prophesied the foundation of a great city, whose glory would touch the stars, on the rocky hill near Strahov forest. Hradčany's commanding view of Prague clearly reveals the strategic value of the site to the princes of the Czech tribes who made it their seat of power from the end of the ninth century. Little remains today of the Castle from which they consolidated their power over Bohemia. It was under the early rulers, however, that Prague Castle (Pražký hrad) was established as the seat of state and religious power. The fortification system built by Prince Bořivoj – the first documented member of the dynasty – towards the end of the ninth century defined the basic layout of the Castle, a stronghold which included the royal residence and church.

Boleslav II (967–99) won the right to found the bishopric of Prague, establishing an independent diocese with institutions of religious and cultural importance to Bohemia. Přemysl Otakar II (1253–78) built himself a new palace, fit for Bohemian kings who had finally won their

When Vladislav Jagiello moved the court back to the Castle from the Old Town, the buildings were in poor repair. One of his first steps was to improve the northern fortifications. Mihulka Tower played an important part in the defence of the Castle. The embrasures for firearms and cannons can still be seen in the tower, which now houses exhibitions on the history of the Castle.

hereditary title from the Holy Roman Emperor. Succeeding dynasties continued to fortify and embellish the complex of buildings, creating a royal settlement with a rich architectural heritage.

Views of the Castle give a good idea of that heritage. Black Tower (Černa věž), to the east, was built in the twelfth century to guard the path through the complex. The fifteenth-century fortifications include the Daliborka, White (Bílá věž) and Mihulka Towers to the north, overlooking the sixteenth-century Royal Garden (Královská zahrada) and Summer Palace (Královsky Letohrádek), while the southern range of the Castle was given its present appearance during the reign of Maria Theresa (1740–80). Behind it rise the Romanesque towers of the Basilica of St George (Bazilika sv Jiří), the Gothic tower of the St Vitus Cathedral (Chrám sv Víta) and its neo-Gothic spires. The range of styles matches the purposes served over the centuries by this complex of buildings as different monarchs used the Castle to assert their status and ambitions. Their building programmes addressed the military, political and religious roles of the Castle, where strategic, regal and ceremonial considerations all played a part in the building projects. The term 'castle' hardly seems to be an adequate description of the resulting town within the town of Hradčany.

Construction work on the Castle progressed in fits and starts according to the availability of funds and the political situation. In addition to Maria Theresa, the names most closely associated with it are those of Charles IV (1346–78), Vladislav Jagiello (1471–1516) and the early Habsburgs, Ferdinand I (1526–64) and Rudolph II (1576–1611). With time and changing military strategy, what had started out as a fortress was converted into a palace fit for Renaissance kings. Ferdinand I took the decision to break away from the confines of the medieval Castle and create the Royal Garden on the other side of the northern moat. Regal splendour was the priority, culminating in the sparkling reign of Rudolph II, the last Habsburg to live in Prague. After 1620 the Castle was more a symbol of power than anything else, as the Habsburgs displayed a marked preference for Vienna. The monarch was only rarely in residence from then on and there was little building activity until Maria Theresa's works in the eighteenth century.

Visitors to the Castle today generally see the more recent buildings first, crossing the first two – rather shallow – courtyards to the heart of the site around the Third Courtyard. The entrance on Hradčany Square

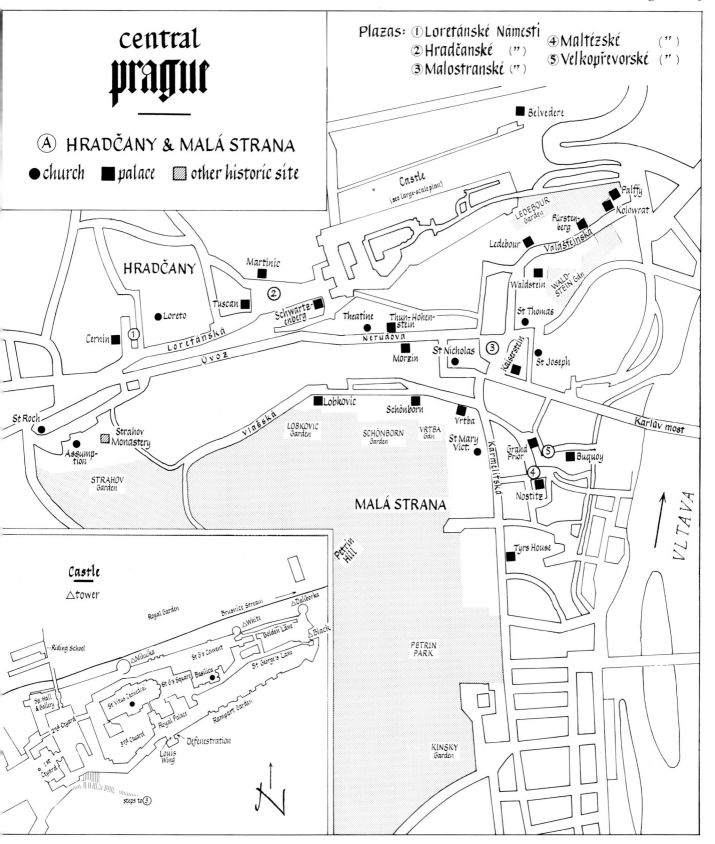

central prague

Ⓐ HRADČANY & MALÁ STRANA

● church　■ palace　▨ other historic site

Plazas: ① Loretánské Námesti
② Hradčanské (")
③ Malostranské (")
④ Maltézské (")
⑤ Velkopřevorské (")

■ Belvedere

Castle (see large-scale plan)

HRADČANY

■ Martinic

LEDEBOUR Garden

Ledebour ■　Valaštejnská

Fürsten-berg ■　Palffy ■
Kolowrat ■

Waldstein ■　WALD-STEIN Gdn

■ Tuscan

● Loreto

② Schwartz-enberg ■

● Theatine

Thun-Hohen-stein ■

St Thomas ●

● Cernin ■　①

Loretánská

ÚVOZ

Nerudova

Morzin ■

St Nicholas ●

③ Kaiserstein ■

St Joseph ●

St Roch ●

Vlašská

■ Lobkovic

LOBKOVIC Garden

Schönborn ■

SCHÖNBORN Garden

VRTBA Gdn

Vrtba ■

St Mary Vict. ●

Karmelitská

Grand Prior ■　⑤

Buquoy ■

Karlův most

● Assump-tion

Strahov Monastery ▨

STRAHOV Garden

MALÁ STRANA

④

Nostitz ■

Tyrs House ■

Petrin Hill

PETRIN PARK

VLTAVA

Castle

△ tower

Royal Garden

Brusnice Stream

△ Daliborka

△ Whitt

Golden Lane

△ Black

~Riding School

△ Mihulka

St G's Convent

St. George's Lane

Sp. Hall & Gallery

2nd Cyard

St Vitus Cathedral ●

St G's Square　Basilica

3rd Cyard

Royal Palace

Rampart Garden

□ 1st Cyard

Defenestration

Louis Wing

steps to ③

KINSKY Garden

N

The Castle viewed from the south: St Vitus Cathedral rises behind the neoclassical range on either side of All Saints Chapel, Vladislav Hall and the Louis Wing, the scene of the 1618 Defenestration of Prague.

The Battling Giants tower over the main entrance to the Castle. Seen here from the Second Courtyard, they are copies of the 1768 sculptures by Ignác František Platzer, commissioned for Nicolo Pacassi's grand entrance to the new First Courtyard.

(Hradčanské náměstí) through the gateway guarded by copies of Ignác Platzer's (1717–87) rather threatening Battling Giants leads into the First Courtyard, or Cour d'honneur, built by the Viennese court architect, Nicolo Pacassi (1716–90) on the site of an earlier moat. It still has a ceremonial role: the changing of the Castle guard takes place every hour and includes trumpeters who appear at the windows overlooking the courtyard. This was one of the few real additions made to the Castle during the extensive rebuilding programme of 1763–71. The work mostly involved recasting the existing buildings as the neoclassical Theresian range.

There is something rather theatrical in the effect of the uniform façades partly obscuring, partly acting as a foil to the buildings within the complex. This is increased by the knowledge that there was very little in the rooms that Pacassi built. This was a provincial palace; there was no reason to furnish it impressively and visitors in the eighteenth century were dismissive of everything except the view. The grounds were not well maintained, many of the buildings were used as barracks and storehouses and the palace was made available to homeless monarchs like the exiled King of France, Charles X. Chateaubriand, visiting him there in 1833, was rather depressed by the dark and unfurnished rooms; the immense castle of the Kings of Bohemia reminded him of the 'terrible monastery of the Escorial'.

Going through the Matthias Gate (Matyášova brána) into the Second Courtyard takes us back further to more splendid times, the days of the first Habsburgs. The 1536 Powder Bridge (Prašný most) over the Stag Moat (Jelení příkop) led into the Royal Garden and the Italianate world of the new dynasty. The garden was a gem of the Northern Renaissance, created as a place of beauty and distraction for the court. Over the years it acquired fountains, ball courts, a shooting gallery, a maze and a menagerie. A number of exotic plants first came to Europe through the orangery and fig garden, a claim to distinction that was to serve the garden well: when Prague was occupied in the 1740s, the commander of the French forces accepted thirty pineapples in exchange for restraining his troops from sacking the grounds.

The major building of the early Habsburg years is the Summer Palace (or Belvedere) at the east end of the Royal Garden. On 13 November 1534, Ferdinand I announced that he had commissioned Italian master builders and masons to build his Summer Palace. By then he was

Emperor as well as King of Bohemia and had moved his court to Vienna. He retained an interest in the Prague Castle, however, as did his regent, Archduke Ferdinand, who oversaw many of the building projects. The Summer Palace with its classical themes marked a new departure in Bohemian architecture, and is the earliest surviving such garden structure in Central Europe.

It was designed by the Genoese architect and sculptor Paolo della Stella who was involved with the project from 1538 until his death in 1552. During that time the ground floor and arcade were completed despite the delays caused by the fire of 1541 that devastated much of Hradčany and the Lesser Quarter. The arcade confirms the Italian inspiration behind the building, with its Ionic order, its tendril frieze and the mythological and hunting scenes in the spandrels. There are over thirty reliefs, carved by della Stella and his team using marble-working techniques on sandstone. The classical motifs used link Ferdinand I and his brother, the Emperor Charles V, with Hercules, Perseus and Cadmos as well as Alexander the Great.

The Belvedere was completed by court architect Boniface Wolmut (d. 1579) between 1556 and 1563. The terrace running above the arcade was inspired by Serlio's published depiction of Bramante's Tempietto in Rome: such theoretical sources were of considerable importance to architects working in Prague from this period onwards. Wolmut also designed the ball courts in the Royal Garden. The small one has disappeared, but the large one with its elegant northern arcade and sgraffito bears witness to the days of courtly diversions.

The reign of Rudolph II is associated less with buildings than with his collections and an ambiguous legacy of learning and Mannerist eccentricity. His reputation was well established by the time the English traveller Fynes Moryson visited Prague in 1591. He reported that the Emperor 'was said to love solitariness, and to exercise the Arts of Alchemy and Painting'. Rudolph II was the last Habsburg to have his court in Prague and he gathered around him in the Castle a number of scientists and artists of international renown: Tycho Brahe (1546–1601) and Johannes Kepler (1571–1630) were his court astronomers; Arcimboldo (1527–93) his court painter; the painter Bartholomeus Spranger (1546–1611) worked for him as did the sculptor Adriaen de Vries (1545–1626). His interest in paintings, *objets d'art*, plants and animals dictated many of his building projects. He had the southern

Matthias Gate, erected in 1614, was the first hint of the Baroque in Prague. It was the western entrance to the Castle until the First Courtyard was built in 1763–71, when the gate was incorporated into the wall between the first two courts.

Above centre & right Buildings under wraps are a common sight in Prague, where restoration is a never-ending process. The sixteenth-century Royal Summer Palace (or Belvedere), built for Prague's first Habsburg king, Ferdinand I, at the eastern edge of his new Royal Garden, is highly prized for is arcades decorated with mythological, historical and genre scenes. Held to be the best example of Italian Renaissance architecture north of the Alps, it has been used as an exhibition hall in recent years.

Overleaf Nicolo Pacassi's new façades transformed the picturesque outlines of the medieval and Renaissance Castle into the neoclassical symmetries of the Theresian range, exemplified in these windows overlooking the Third Courtyard.

wing of the palace rebuilt and added the buildings between the Second and Third Courtyards as well as the Spanish Hall and Gallery above the Spanish Stables – the buildings that now house the Castle Gallery (Obrazárna Pražského hradu).

Not much of Rudolph II's collection is to be seen there today. At the close of the Thirty Years War in 1648 the Swedish army occupied the Castle, Hradčany and the Lesser Quarter. While they caused considerable damage all over Prague, they have gone down in history for looting a number of palaces and making off with the bulk of Rudolph's collection. Paintings, statues, books and other treasures – including a lion from the menagerie – were loaded on to five barges and shipped to Queen Christina. As a result of her later abdication and move to Rome the paintings were further dispersed; the presence of works chosen by the eccentric monarch for his Prague collection in museums throughout the world is often read by commentators on the history of Prague as entirely in keeping with the confiscation, exile and death that followed the crushing of the Bohemian rebellion against the Habsburgs in 1620.

The combined effects of the 1541 fire and the growing needs of the court encouraged the early Habsburgs to continue the westward extension of the residential palace in the Third Courtyard, started by Vladislav Jagiello after he moved the court back to Hradčany from the Old Town in 1483. The designer of Vladislav's modern fortifications, Benedikt Ried (1451–1534), was also involved in modernizing his palace. In his greatest contribution to the palace, Ried used the outer walls of the upper rooms to build one of the largest medieval secular halls in Europe, Vladislav Hall, which features the crowning glory of Gothic architecture in the Castle in its remarkable vaulting, and in its windows signals the Renaissance forms to come.

> The hall of the palace measures two hundred and twelve feet in length and thirty feet in width. Above it has an artful vault and there is no column in the centre upon which it would rest. The floor or pavement is of such thickness that several troops of cavalry can ride about and engage in chivalrous games there . . .
> (*Itinerarium Germanium*, Marinus Zeiler, 1632)

The vaulting here contrasts sharply with the decorative net-vaulting in the ground floor hall that was restored by Ried's predecessors: the ribs curve up the supporting piers and are gathered into six-pointed rosettes

articulating the vast space. The empty hall is a beautiful room that served a variety of purposes in the past. It was built as the Big Hall of Homage used for coronation banquets, meetings of the Estates, tournaments and, during the reign of Rudolph II, sales of luxury goods and works of art.

The explanation for the difference between the dynamism of the hall interior and the elegance of the Renaissance windows lies in Vladislav's move to Hungary in 1490 when he succeeded Matthias Corvinus and inherited his modern residence at Buda Castle. Hungary had early contacts with Italian builders, many of whom moved to Bohemia after the Hungarian court was occupied by the Turks early in the sixteenth century. Vladislav Jagiello was eager to follow the Hungarian example, and the later Louis Wing of the Royal Palace is Renaissance in feel.

The Louis Wing – named for Vladislav's son and heir – was originally residential. After the fire of 1541 it housed offices, including the Bohemian Chancellery, the supreme administrative body of the kingdom. That was how it came to be the site of the most famous instance of Prague's way of dealing with recalcitrant officialdom: defenestration. Two Catholic governors and their clerk were thrown out of a first-floor window on 23 May 1618, marking the beginning of the rebellion of the Estates against Habsburg rule. The spot where they landed – and picked themselves up – is now marked by two obelisques.

Vladislav Jagiello rebuilt the palace because much of what had been done during the reign of Charles IV was in ruins by the late fifteenth century: the Castle had not been spared during the Hussite Wars. Charles IV himself had found similar devastation on his return from the French court in 1333. There is little sign now of the buildings which the Emperor himself described in his autobiography: 'The Castle of Prague was completely deserted, ruined and destroyed, for since the reign of King Otakar II it had been wrecked to the ground. On that place we had a large and beautiful palace built anew at considerable cost, as passers-by today can witness . . .' (Vita Caroll).

The best visual record of the Golden Age of Prague under Charles IV is St Vitus Cathedral, the culmination of the church-building tradition begun by the early Přemyslids. While Prince Bořivoj had the first church built within the Castle precinct, his grandson Wenceslas (921–9) is the ruler whose name is most closely associated with early Christianity in the kingdom. He was sanctified after his murder by his brother, and as

Vladislav Hall is 62 metres long, 16 metres wide and 13 metres high; it takes up the space of the second floor of Charles IV's palace. The vault is borne by six pairs of pillars partly built into the walls. Originally used for coronation festivities and tournaments as well as assemblies, it has retained a ceremonial function.

The Milanese painter Giuseppe Arcimboldo was court painter in Prague from 1562 to 1587. He worked as portraitist, copyist and Master of Court Festivals and Masquerades. He is best known now for his fantastical composite paintings of heads, made up of plants, fruits and vegetables. His portrait of Rudolph II (*c.* 1590), with his mulberry and cherry eyes, melon forehead, pear nose and peach and apple cheeks, was a fitting tribute to the Mannerist ruler. It was seized as booty, along with much of the royal collection, by the Swedish troops who occupied Prague in 1648 at the close of the Thirty Years War. Courtesy Skoklosters Slott, Stockholm.

patron saint of Bohemia his legendary efforts to unite the kingdom and bring about political and religious independence made him a central figure invoked not only by those who ruled after him but by the people of Bohemia as well.

It was in 973 that one of Wenceslas's ambitions was realized. Pope John XIII founded the independent bishopric for which he had campaigned. The diocese not only enjoyed independence from the diocese of Regensburg, it also acquired institutions of cultural significance. The Convent of Benedictine Nuns at the Church of St George (Klášter sv Jiří) produced a number of important illuminated manuscripts in the Middle Ages, and now houses the National Gallery's collection of medieval art. When the convent was built, the older Basilica of St George was enlarged. Its present appearance is due to restoration of its Romanesque interior and Baroque western façade which was undertaken at the turn of the century. The juxtaposition in styles is a feature of Prague's ecclesiastical architecture; the basilica also has a beautiful Renaissance south doorway.

Wenceslas had built the rotunda of St Vitus in anticipation of making Prague an independent bishopric. It was replaced in the eleventh century by a basilica consecrated to St Wenceslas, St Vitus and St Adalbert. In 1344 Charles IV decided to build on that site a cathedral worthy of the new archdiocese of Prague. However, as the building developed it came to be more a statement of personal power than a celebration of the newly won independence from the Archbishop of Mainz. His Cathedral of St Vitus is the product of his education at the French court, his ties to the Bohemia of his mother and a vision of his imperial capital that was to determine the appearance of much of Prague.

Charles IV turned to France for his first architect, Matthias of Arras (d. 1352), the master-mason of Narbonne Cathedral. Matthias established a lodge at the Castle that became a centre for foreign architects working in Bohemia. His work on the Cathedral recalls the regular, geometric forms of French cathedrals; by the time he died he had completed the ground floor of the choir and eight out of ten apsidal chapels. The work was continued by Peter Parler (1330–99), from Swabian Gmünd, whose design, harnessed to Charles IV's dynastic programme, makes for the striking beauty of the building. Parler's rich decorative scheme and unification of the choir space – net-vaulting as opposed to separately vaulted bays – contrast with the more austere forms of his predecessor. He was responsible for the South Portal, the South Tower and Wenceslas Chapel. This part of St Vitus faces the Royal Palace, confirming the extent to which it was the Emperor's Cathedral. The setting for royal coronations and burials came to take precedence over the central sanctuary of the Bohemian church.

The chapels in St Vitus house the tombs of Charles IV's Přemyslid ancestors, and the Chapel of St Wenceslas was built on the site of the saint's earlier rotunda. The iconographic scheme of the Cathedral rests heavily on the continuity of that dynasty. Charles IV himself is very present in his Cathedral: in the mosaic of the Last Judgment over the South Portal and as donor in the wall-painting above the altar in the Chapel of St Wenceslas, he appears alongside the patron saints of Bohemia. In the remarkable portrait busts in the lower triforium his likeness appears with members of his family, the builders of the Cathedral and first archbishops of Prague; above them in the upper triforium the patron saints, Christ and the Virgin stand guard over the Přemyslids, the Luxemburgs and their works.

Little was done over the centuries to complete Charles IV's Cathedral: the Hussite Wars intervened, then other wars, other priorities. After the Habsburgs moved their court away from Prague, St Vitus was the focus of what life the Castle retained, as coronation ceremonies were held there. In the 1720s additional ceremonies were held in the Cathedral, for the beatification and sanctification of St John Nepomuk, a saint much favoured by the Habsburgs in their re-Catholicization of their Bohemian kingdom. In 1736 the saint's extravagant silver tomb was placed in the Cathedral. In the course of the century it was surrounded by statues of Justice, Strength, Wisdom and Reticence and four silver angels holding up a baldachine: St John here is vying not just with John Huss, whose memory he was to supplant, but also with St Wenceslas and his chapel studded with semi-precious stones.

The fabric of the building was hardly touched, however. It was not until the nineteenth century that anyone took any interest in the history, conservation or completion of the Cathedral. By then both St Vitus and the Castle as a whole had come to be of great significance to nationalists who felt that they were the spiritual heirs of St Wenceslas and Charles IV: it was under the auspices of the 1859 Association for

Golden Lane is one of the Castle's most popular sights. Its tiny houses, squeezed up against the northern fortifications between White Tower and Daliborka Tower, originally housed Castle guards and craftsmen, including goldsmiths – but not Rudolph II's alchemists, despite the legend to that effect. The houses were built in the late sixteenth century and were inhabited until the 1950s. Franz Kafka had the use of No 22 during the winter of 1916–17; he wrote there all night and walked to his room in the Old Town to sleep. The house has recently been acquired by Prague's new Kafka Society, which plans to open a bookshop there, alongside the little antique and souvenir shops on the lane. Manifest interest in Kafka's work is one of the many changes ushered in by the Velvet Revolution of November 1989. The dissident playwright, Václav Havel – pictured in the Golden Lane window – was one of the leaders of the opposition movement, Civic Forum. One of the cries heard regularly during the revolution was *Havel na Hrad!* (Havel to the Castle!): he is now President of the Republic and occupies the state offices in the Castle.

Left The Basilica of St George is one of the oldest churches in Prague. It was founded in the tenth century by Prince Vratislav I and the main nave still has its original arcades. The church was rebuilt in 1142 after a fire: the crypt and towers date from that period, whereas the Early Baroque western façade was added in the seventeenth century. The adjoining Chapel of St John Nepomuk was built between 1717 and 1722. Research and restoration carried out this century led to the recovery of the original appearance of the interior. The church is now used as a concert hall.

Above right This Late Gothic relief of St George and the Dragon decorating the southern portal of the Basilica of St George is a copy of the original carving, now in the National Gallery.

Below right St George makes another appearance in this copy of a 1373 equestrian statue in the Third Courtyard; the original is in the St. George's Convent Museum in the Castle.

Left St Wenceslas Chapel in St Vitus Cathedral was built in 1362–7 by Peter Parler, the second architect to work on the Cathedral for Charles IV. The lavishly decorated chapel was built on the site of the tenth century rotunda where the saint was buried. St Wenceslas is central to the decorative scheme of the chapel: in addition to this tomb, it includes his statue by Peter Parler and the early sixteenth-century paintings on the upper walls depicting his life and miracles. The lower cycle of paintings, devoted to the life of Christ, is studded with semi-precious stones.

Above right Building began on St Vitus Cathedral in 1344, after Prague had become an independent archdiocese. The eastern section of the building was consecrated in 1385 and given a temporary wall when the Hussite Wars disrupted work after 1415. While construction resumed in the late fifteenth century it was not until 1929 that St Vitus was completed: the Neo-Gothic western façade and nave vaulting date from the final building phase. The names most closely associated with the cathedral are those of Charles IV and his architects, Matthias of Arras and Peter Parler, responsible for the choir, its chapels and the grand south façade with its tower and Golden Portal.

Below right The Cathedral's Golden Portal mosaic of the Last Judgment was executed in 1370 by North Italian artists. Charles IV and his consort, Elizabeth of Pomerania, are portrayed kneeling below the patron saints of Bohemia.

Above The Old Castle Steps lead up to the Observation Terrace and the eastern entrance to the Castle. The ceremony surrounding the changing of the guard, both here and at the entrance on Hradčany Square, regularly attracts onlookers.

Below Hradčany Square, 70 metres above the Vltava, was the centre of the town of Hradčany, founded in 1320. There was much new building there after the fire of 1541, when many aristocrats decided to settle at the Castle gates. Many of the Renaissance palaces were substantially altered in the eighteenth and nineteenth centuries.

the Completion of the Cathedral of St Vitus that Prague began to atone for the neglect of the Habsburg court. Work was well under way when the Czechoslovak Republic was proclaimed in 1918 and the Castle became the official residence of the head of state, thus recapturing the full significance of its history.

The Town

The history of Hradčany itself is bound up with that of the Castle. It was the Castle burgrave who in 1320 granted the community on the outer bailey the status of a town under his authority. The settlement originally reached a little beyond what is now Hradčany Square; it was extended as far as Strahov Monastery (Strahovský klášter) during the reign of Charles IV. Proximity to the Castle was of course a major attraction for those whose lives revolved around the court. The Rozmberk and Lobkowic families actually built their palaces within the Castle precinct; others had to settle for family burial vaults in St Vitus Cathedral and palaces in Hradčany – or the Lesser Quarter.

Relations between Castle and Estates were not always easy. After the 1541 fire, the rumour spread that Ferdinand I himself had started it because he wished to put to the torch the archives documenting the historic rights of the nobility, gentry and burghers as well as the 1526 electoral proceedings in which he had agreed to respect the freedom of religion of his largely Protestant kingdom. Matters were put to the test shortly afterwards when he wanted to raise forces to go to the aid of Emperor Charles V in his confrontation with the Protestant princes of the Holy Roman Empire. The Bohemians were inclined to support their co-religionists: they lost the ensuing battle. Ferdinand I's reprisals concentrated on the royal towns, which lost many privileges, and on the more radical Hussite group, the Bohemian Brethren. The aristocracy was spared in this first clash; two members of the gentry and two burghers were executed on Hradčany Square.

Hradčany's present-day appearance dates back to the period following the fire when a number of ambitious palaces were built on the ruins of older houses. It was Jan of Lobkowic who acquired the site of Schwarzenberg Palace after the fire. The sgraffito decoration – echoing that on the buildings being erected in the Royal Garden – gables and cornice lunettes were typical of Renaissance architecture in Bohemia.

Recent restoration work on Martinic Palace has revealed biblical and mythological sgraffito decoration on the façades: the interest in Italian style is linked to the teams of Italian architects working for the court. Whereas the Renaissance buildings show emulation of what was happening within the Castle, the later palaces, churches and monasteries show the extent to which the initiative passed on to the nobility and the Church in the seventeenth and eighteenth centuries.

The Frenchman Jean-Baptiste Mathey (1630–96) had been a painter in the Poussin circle before training as an architect in Rome. He was brought to Prague by Johann Friedrich, Count Waldstein on his appointment as archbishop in 1675. Mathey is credited with introducing a note of restraint in his buildings that compares favourably with the sometimes heavy-handed Early Baroque churches and palaces of Prague. Troja Palace, summer residence for the Sternberg family, on the outskirts of Prague and the Church of St Francis (Kostel sv Františka) in the Old Town are the best examples of his classical, French approach. The Hradčany palace he designed for the Archbishop was rebuilt in the eighteenth century; all that remains of the earlier building is the main portal and the chapel decoration. Mathey also designed Tuscan Palace, for Michael Oswald Thun-Hohenstein, as well as the Castle Riding School.

Facing each other across Loreto Square (Loretánské náměstí) are two buildings that are extreme examples of architectural developments in Prague in the wake of the victory of the Catholic forces of the Habsburgs in 1620. Černín Palace and the Loreto (Loreta) give some idea of the ambitions of aristocracy and Church in Baroque Prague. The palace was built between 1668 and 1688 for Humprech Jan Černín, the imperial ambassador to Venice, who had returned with a considerable art collection. It was designed by the North Italian architect Francesco Caratti (d. 1677); his orders were apparently to outdo the Leopold range of the Vienna Hofburg, and the Emperor was not best pleased when he saw the monumental 150-metre façade with its basement diamond rustication and 30 giant engaged columns.

The Loreto is a much more graceful building, one of fifty shrines built in Bohemia during the Counter-Reformation on the model of the Italian Casa Santa, the house of the Holy Family believed to have been rescued stone by stone from Jerusalem. Countess Benigna Katharina of Lobkowic laid the foundation stone of the central chapel in 1626; the

Above In 1626, Countess Katerina of Lobkowic commissioned a copy of the Santa Casa in Loreto, Italy. The chapel, built by Giovanni Domenico Orsi, is at the heart of the complex of buildings within the cloisters of the Prague Loreto. The façade – of which a detail is shown here – was built by Kilián Dientzenhofer in 1720–2; Ondřej Philip Quintainer was responsible for the sculptural decoration. The Loreto attracted many pilgrims and played a significant part in the re-Catholicization of Bohemia after the defeat of the Protestants at the Battle of White Mountain on 8 November 1620.

Below A detail of the diamond rustication of Černín Palace (1668–88), the residence designed by Francesco Caratti for Count Humprecht Jan Černín. The monumental Palladian palace with its thirty engaged columns was an early example of the use of the architectural orders in Prague. The façade was damaged during the French occupation of 1742; it acquired its three portals and balcony in the subsequent restoration.

Nový Svět was originally a poor quarter of Hradčany. The picturesque cottages date back to 1600, though their present appearance is due to rebuilding carried out in the eighteenth and nineteenth centuries.

The name Pohořelec ('Scene of Fire') refers to the devastation of this part of Hradčany during the Hussite Wars, the fire of 1541 and the French occupation of 1742. Many of the houses were rebuilt in Baroque style after the last catastrophe.

Schwarzenberg Palace (1547–67) on Hradčany Square, overlooking the Lesser Quarter, is one of the most imposing buildings in Prague. The gables, projecting lunette cornice and bold sgraffito decoration were all features of Bohemian Renaissance palace architecture. The palace now houses the Museum of Military History.

stucco reliefs of Old Testament prophets and scenes from the life of the Virgin were added in 1664. The shrine also includes the Church of the Nativity (Kostel Narození Páně), which was begun by the celebrated Bavarian architect, Christoph Dientzenhofer (1655–1722). Christoph's son, Kilián Ignac (1689–1751), unified the complex of buildings with the 1721 façade and the two-storey cloister. The cult of the Virgin Mary and the saints were an important part of the re-Catholicization process in Bohemia. As a place of pilgrimage, the Loreto was given a number of valuable gifts over the years: these votive offerings are on display in the Treasury and include some remarkable Baroque pieces, most famously the diamond monstrance, a sunburst of 6500 of the precious stones.

Hradčany is a very grand place. That grandeur is not solely due to the impressive buildings in themselves, their beautifully restored state or the spaciousness that is in contrast to the other towns. The very setting of the buildings on the crest of the hill dominating Prague imparts a feeling that nothing dominates this town. The feeling is brought home by a walk through the grounds of Strahov Monastery. The Baroque gateway leads past the Church of St Roch (Kostel sv Rocha), the Philosophical and Theological Halls with their impressive libraries, the Church of the Assumption (Kostel Nanebevzetí Panny Marie) and the conventual buildings themselves. Another gate leads out to the monastery gardens; following the path brings all of Prague into sight, in the only view of both banks of the Vltava: the red-tiled roofs of the Lesser Quarter, the dome and tower of the Lesser Quarter St Nicholas Church (Kostel sv Mikuláše), the Charles Bridge (Karlův most), the spires of the Old Town, all appear, followed by the black and white façade of Schwarzenberg Palace and then the Castle itself.

2 The Lesser Quarter (Malá Strana)

After the tempest of God's wrath shall have passed the rule of thy country will again return unto thee, O Czech people.
  Testament, Comenius (1592–1670)

That part of the City, which is situated beyond the River, and commonly called the lesser side, is much more delightful and scarce any thing else is to be seen there but sumptuous palaces, which amount to the number of above three hundred; so that this Quarter may well be styl'd the Magazine of the riches of *Bohemia*, and of his Imperial Majesty's Hereditary Countries.
  The Travels of Charles Patin M.D. of the Faculty of Paris
  (London, 1696)

The House at the Three Ostriches advertises the wares of the ostrich feather merchant who had it rebuilt and decorated in 1606. The first coffee house in Prague was opened here in 1714; the building is now a hotel and restaurant.

Whereas elswhere in Prague there is a remarkable range of architectural styles, the dominant note of the Lesser Quarter is Baroque. This is the site of the Counter-Reformation in Prague; the palaces, those of Catholic loyalists who benefited from the upheavals following the defeat of White Mountain; the churches, those of the religious orders that descended to bring the kingdom back into the fold. The buildings echo the dramatic message of the Church triumphant that we associate with High Baroque Rome. Their splendid presence on the narrow streets nestled between Hradčany, Petřín Hill and the Vltava gives the Lesser Quarter a charm that has appealed to residents and visitors for a very long time.

The street plan of the Lesser Quarter considerably predates the buildings. The town was founded in 1257 by Přemysl Otokar II and extended during the reign of Charles IV: parts of the fourteenth-century fortifications can still be seen on Petřín Hill. Nerudova Street, the main axis of the town, leads up to the Castle and was part of the coronation route. Its proximity to Hradčany attracted aristocrats and wealthy burghers from the sixteenth century onwards. The juxtaposition of Estates and Crown on the left bank of the Vltava gave topographical shape to the conflict between them as the Bohemian Estates sought to defend their privileges against Habsburg incursions.

The town square was of course of central importance to the Lesser

The Lutheran Church of the
Holy Trinity was granted to the
Carmelite Order in 1624. The
new owners had it rebuilt and
reconsecrated as Our Lady of the
Victories: the portal to the right
of the façade is all that remains
of the original church.

The Church of St Nicholas in the
Lesser Quarter is one of the most
celebrated landmarks in Prague.
It was built for the Jesuits by
Christoph and Kilián
Dientzenhofer in two stages:
1704–11 and 1737–55.
Christoph Dientzenhofer's

façade, dominating the Lesser
Quarter Square, is a virtuoso
display of the undulations,
convex and concave forms, and
contrasts of light and shade
associated with High Baroque
architecure.

Jan Lukáš Kracker decorated the nave of St Nicholas in 1760. His Celebration of St Nicholas is one of the largest frescoes in Europe. *Trompe l'oeil* architectural detail links the painting with the nave, while the vitality of the work contributes to the dynamism of the church interior.

Quarter. All three of the town halls that served the town over the generations stood in the market place of the early settlers. The present one dates back to the end of the fifteenth century. The Estates met there in 1575 in order to draft the Bohemian Confession, the basis for future negotiations on the rights of the different groups of Bohemian Protestants to freedom of worship and control of their Church. Emperor Maximilian (1564–76), whose reign was one of relative tolerance, gave his verbal consent to the document. His son Rudolf II granted the 1609 Letter of Majesty establishing the Estates' control of the University and Consistory and their entitlement to 30 Defenders of Protestant rights. This was less a matter of principle than of political expediency: in the face of the Turkish threat and the rivalry of his brother Matthias, the Emperor was in no position to take on the two-thirds of his subjects who were Protestant.

It was under Ferdinand II (1618–37) that the confrontation took place. Elected in the absence of a convincing alternative, he had little intention of abiding by the Letter of Majesty. He had made his position clear as Archduke of Styria, declaring that he would rather rule a ruined country than a damned one. Following a vow to Pope Clement VIII to restore the true faith in his lands, he expelled the Protestants and ruthlessly promoted the Catholic Church. His attitude towards his Bohemian subjects was to prove equally intransigent.

On 22 May 1618, a meeting was held at the home of Albert Smiřický in the Lesser Quarter Square (Malostranské náměstí): the Estates were angered by the appointment of Catholic councillors to the Bohemian Chancellery and by a dispute over the right to build two churches on what Ferdinand II claimed was Catholic land. The following day there was a march on the Castle, where the famous Defenestration occurred. Thirty-six 'Directors' were appointed by the rebels, and a national militia established under Count Thurn. On 26 August 1619, the Directors chose a new ruler, the Calvinist Elector Palatine, Frederick V, who arrived in Prague in October.

The reign of Frederick V, the Winter King, did not even last one season. The Defenestration of Prague was an aristocratic rebellion relying more on outside assistance than popular support. There was little help forthcoming: the putative allies' contribution was mockingly described by the enemy: 'The King of Denmark will send 100 000 red herrings, the Hollanders 100 000 cheeses, and the King of England

Above, right and overleaf
Scenes from the Lesser Quarter.

100 000 ambassadors.' King Frederick was defeated by the imperial forces at the Battle of White Mountain on 8 November 1620. Ferdinand II pressed home his advantage mercilessly. Heeding the urging of Catholic advisers and the Book of Psalms – 'Thou shalt break them with a rod of iron; thou shalt dash them in pieces like a potter's vessel' – he set about imposing his will on his recalcitrant subjects.

Break them he did: there were executions in the Old Town Square in June 1621. Loyal advisers, officers and noblemen were granted land confiscated from the Protestants; vast tracts were sold to the highest bidder, and a new aristocracy was formed. Nearly half of Bohemia came under new ownership in this way. It was decreed that all Protestant ministers had to leave the country and in 1627 people were faced with the choice of Catholicism or exile. One hundred and fifty thousand Bohemians left for Hungary, Poland, the Netherlands or England. Thirty thousand of them were from Prague where the population fell drastically. The exiles were replaced by loyalists to the Crown eager to take advantage of easy access to land and titles. The way had been cleared for a refashioning of Prague: churches were reconsecrated and palaces changed hands. To the new owners, building was an opportunity to assert their power.

There are therefore a number of points to bear in mind when contemplating the secular and religious buildings of the Lesser Quarter. There is an edge to its architectural history: overlying more familiar factors like tradition, innovation, style and taste, there is a sense that the Baroque palaces and churches were the fruit of a defeat, built by patrons who looked towards Rome and Vienna not just for inspiration but also for legitimacy. These owners were doing more than expanding on the Baroque theme that had made its timid beginnings in the four towns: the number and ambition of their projects were such that the Lesser Quarter came to bear the stamp of a new, foreign order. In time, Prague came to make a significant contribution of its own to European High Baroque but it took some time for the gulf between the new order and the land to be bridged. It was the rupture in Bohemian culture, as much as the depredations of war that lie behind the *cri de coeur* of the Jesuit Bohuslav Balbín(1621–88): 'you have utterly destroyed our home, our ancient kingdom, and have built us no new one in its place' (1670).

Church property changed hands immediately after White Mountain.

Far left In 1623, work began on the Early Baroque palace of Albrecht Waldstein, the wealthy and powerful imperial generalissimo during the Thirty Years War. The extent of his Early Baroque palace, with its five courtyards, *sala terrena* and formal gardens, is best appreciated from the Castle Observation Terrace. The palace remained in Waldstein family hands until 1945; it now belongs to the Ministry of Culture.

Left Michna Palace (Tyrš House) illustrates trends in Lesser Quarter architectural history. It was originally a summer palace belonging to the Kinský family: the façade on Újezd Street still has traces of Renaissance sgraffito decoration. It changed hands after the Battle of White Mountain in 1620. The new owner, Pavel Michna and his son Vaclav, had a new Early Baroque east wing built by Francesco Caratti. The garden sweeping down to Kampa Island was added by the Schwarzenbergs in 1684. A century later, the palace was used as an armoury and fell into disrepair. It underwent reconstruction after it was acquired by the Sokol movement in 1921 and the garden was converted into a sports ground. The palace now belongs to the Charles University Sports Faculty; the former Kinský palace houses the Museum of Physical Culture and Sports.

The Church of the Holy Trinity is a good case in point. It was built between 1611 and 1614, as a German Lutheran Church. In 1624 it was granted to the Carmelites who set about rebuilding it in 1640. It was subsequently reconsecrated as St Mary the Victorious (Panny Marie Vítězné) in honour of the triumph at White Mountain. The change took place relatively early in the development of Prague Baroque, which accounts for the flat, austere appearance of St Mary's rather ill-proportioned façade. Ironically enough, the church became a major Catholic shrine. In 1628, Princess Polyxena Lobkowic presented the friary with the 'Christ Child Of Prague' – a family heirloom that her mother had brought with her from Spain – now venerated by Catholics throughout the world.

The later Church of St Joseph (Kostel sv Josefa) was built for the Carmelites between 1687 and 1692, according to some sources by Jean-Baptiste Mathey. The elliptical domed space opening up on to three niches on the longer sides of the oval reflects Baroque experiments in centralizing longitudinal ground plans. Liturgy took priority over theory during the Catholic Reformation, and the centralized plans favoured by the Renaissance were abandoned as impractical for clergy and congregation. The façade has an assertive, sculptural presence that represents a considerable advance on that of St Mary's. Around the corner from St Joseph's, Kilián Dientzenhofer's High Baroque façade for the earlier Church of St Thomas (Kostel sv Tomáše), with its undulations and broken pediment, is an even bolder statement of the interest in making church exteriors a part of the townscape.

Christoph and Kilián Dientzenhofer were both associated with the Jesuit Lesser Quarter Church of St Nicholas, one of the most famous of Prague landmarks. The vertical note of the church dome and tower against the prevailing horizontal lines of the Lesser Quarter was Kilián Dientzenhofer's stroke of genius: commissioned to complete his father's work, he made a dramatic contribution to the city skyline.

The Jesuits acquired a number of properties in the Lesser Quarter after White Mountain. The former Jesuit College in the middle of the Square occupies the site of twenty houses. The church that they commissioned after the college is their most ambitious one in Bohemia. The original plans were for a longitudinal, single-nave church reminiscent of Il Gesù, their church in Rome. It is thought that Christoph Dientzenhofer introduced the changes that make the nave such a dynamic space. Its rhythmic articulation is reminiscent of designs by the Turin architect Guarino Guarini (1624–83), whose designs, published in his *Architecture civile* of 1686, were influential in Bohemia. Guarini, himself a Theatine father, designed a Prague church for his order but his plans were not used. Christoph Dientzenhofer was one of the first architects working in Bohemia to be inspired by the Italian's complex spatial arrangements.

St Nicholas is an overwhelming church; its effects are those of persuasion and edification, in keeping with Jesuit appeals to the imagination and the senses. The angled piers, undulating gallery, soaring figure of St Nicholas and towering statues of Jesuit saints and virtues propel the viewer forward to the choir where a further proliferation of architectural and sculptural elements cluster in the area beneath the dome. The play of light on the interior marbling, the constant visual stimulation, the sheer multiplication of effects in a space designed to enhance them demonstrate the full force of Baroque theatricality that is only partly achieved by the lavish 'Barocization' of older churches.

Though the foundations for the church were laid in 1673, building did not begin until 1703. By 1711 the nave had been vaulted and the façade completed, but the east end was closed off by a wooden screen until the second building phase began in 1737. That was when Kilián Dientzenhofer took the decision to change his father's design for the choir and sacristy. The high drum and tower, each 79 metres high, were completed in 1755 and the interior frescoes in 1761.

Of the secular landowners in Bohemia, Albrecht von Waldstein (1583–1634) was one of the first to see the opportunities afforded by the Habsburgs. A convert to Catholicism in 1606, he was part of Ferdinand's retinue before the Archduke's election to the Bohemian throne. His Jesuit confessor arranged his marriage to Lucretia Neksova, a wealthy widow who died leaving him her fortune, which he invested in land that had been confiscated from the rebels of 1618. By 1623 he owned close to a quarter of Bohemia. The following year work began on his Prague palace. Accounts vary as to how many properties were swallowed up in the process of building a residence fit for the man who had become Generalissimo of the Imperial Armies of the Thirty Years War, and Military Governor of Prague, but at least 25 houses, three gardens and a town gate were destroyed to provide the site facing the Castle.

In the days before house numbers, Prague residences had names; homeowners put up decorative signs so that they could be located. The decorative signs outside houses like At The Swan (49/232 Nerudova Street) or At The Three Storks (16/20 Tomášska Street) hark back to that tradition. The signs sometimes point to the owner's occupation: At The Three Violins (12/210 Nerudova Street) was once the home of a family of violin makers, and a goldsmith lived in At the Golden Cup (No 16/212 Nerudova Street).

Given Waldstein's larger-than-life career, it is not surprising to find hyperbolic accounts of the palace including references to hundreds of retainers, gorgeously attired attendants and descriptions evocative of his wealth and power:

> His stables contained upwards of 1000 saddle and carriage horses, which fed out of marble troughs. When he travelled, there were never less than fifty carriages, drawn by six horses, and fifty drawn by four. In a lofty vaulted banqueting-hall of his palace at Prague, he was depicted in a triumphal car, drawn by four horses of the sun, with a star over his laurel crowned head. The long suites or rooms in this palace were filled with astrological, allegorical, and mythological figures. A secret staircase led from a small round saloon into a grotto of artificial stalactites where there was a bath. Adjoining this grotto was a spacious portico; from which one entered the gardens, adorned with fountains and with canals abounding with fish.
>
> (*Memoirs of the Court of Austria*, Karl Eduard Vehse, London 1856)

Like the other Early Baroque buildings in Prague, Waldstein Palace was the work of architects and artists of the North Italian school. Andrea Spezza (d. 1628) drew up the original plans and Baccio di Bianco (1604–56) painted the hall frescoes. In its mass and articulation, external austerity and lavish interior decoration, Waldstein's palace is typical of its period, though its extent is exceptional. The elegant Italian formal gardens are open to the public during the summer; they have retained their grottoes, ponds, aviary and an arcaded *sala terrena*. The bronze statues are copies of the originals by Adriaen de Vries: the originals were carried off as war booty by the Swedes in 1648.

By then, Waldstein himself was dead; he was murdered in 1634 after Ferdinand II discovered the final intrigue of his insatiably ambitious commander-in-chief. Not satisfied with the land and wealth he had amassed during the Thirty Years War while doing battle for the Emperor in the name of the Counter-Reformation, he had been engaged in secret negotiations with the enemy and had demanded an oath of allegiance from his generals on 12 January 1634. The loss of Waldstein severely affected Ferdinand II's chances of reimposing Catholicism on the German princes. However, there was little comfort for the Bohemian exiles in the concessions made by his successor Ferdinand III

Giovanni Santini designed a new façade for Václav Morzin's Nerudova Street palace in 1713–14. He worked with the sculptor Ferdinand Maximilian Brokoff, whose Moors supporting the balcony are a good example of the marriage of the arts in Baroque Prague.

(1637–57) in the Peace of Prague (1635) or the Peace of Westphalia (1648): they could still return only if they recanted. Ironically, the Waldstein Palace now houses a museum dedicated to one of the most celebrated of those who had to flee, John Amos Comenius (1592–1670), the Bohemian Brethren minister and influential educationalist.

Other seventeenth-century projects in the Lesser Quarter were more modest. The new owners rarely acquired vast tracts of land and often chose to have existing buildings modernized rather than starting from scratch. Where the site permitted, extensions were built. In 1625 Pavel Michna Vacinov, who had made his fortune in the war, acquired the Thurn family's summer palace now known as Tyrš House. His son Václav, eager to emulate Waldstein, also turned to the Italian community for his architect; Francesco Caratti designed a new east wing for the Renaissance palace.

Caratti, originally from Como, was part of a group of architects who had settled in the Italian community of the Lesser Quarter during the reign of Rudolph II. In 1617 these architects built the Casa d'Italia and the Church of St Charles Borromeo on Vlašská (Italian) Street. Caratti himself is associated with a number of Early Baroque buildings in Prague in addition to Tyrš House, notably Černín Palace and Nostic Palace. He and Carlo Lurago (c. 1618–84) were among the most successful of those continuing the tradition of the Comasques who had been coming to Prague since the sixteenth century. These buildings all reflect the continuing influence of the Italian architects in Central Europe. The breakdown of the imperial guild system during the Thirty Years War and the vast amount of reconstruction to be done meant that their lodges, which dealt with every aspect of building from design to interior decoration, were much in demand after 1650.

The early palaces share a certain monumental grandeur: long, impressive façades, strong horizontal lines articulated by giant orders. Černín Palace is famous for its series of engaged columns, while it was Nostic Palace that first used the Palladian colossal order. Caratti's building was altered later: the monotony of the façade is now relieved by the eighteenth-century doorway, dormer windows and statues of emperors that reflect the shift in taste associated with the High Baroque in Prague. Patrons moved away from the rather rigid symmetries of the Comasque school and became increasingly interested in new developments in Italy. It was often discouraging to try to obtain the services of

Above The Giovanni Santini façade of Thun-Hohenstein Palace incorporates two giant eagles with curved, outspread wings: the heraldic emblems of Norbert Vincenc of Kolowrat who had the work done 1721–6. They were designed by Matthias Bernard Braun, referred to as the 'Bohemian Bernini' because of the dynamism of his work.

Right Colourful sights in the Lesser Quarter.

Left Detail of the façade decoration of the House at the Three Ostriches.

Above right Buquoy Palace on Grand Priory Square is now the French Embassy. It has been repainted recently and its bright colour contrasts strongly with the weathered tones of its neighbours. There is some controversy about the use of modern paint on historic buildings as it does not reproduce the effects of traditional materials.

Below right The ornate Baroque façade of At the Two Standard Bearers is decorated with a framed painting of a Madonna and Child. The plaque indicates that the writer and translater František Doucha (1810–84) once lived here.

the masters themselves so those architects who were directly or indirectly familiar with the work of Bernini, Borromini, Guarini and others stepped into the breach. From 1700 men like Santini, Alliprandi, Kaňka and the Dientzenhofers dominated the scene.

The architects working in Prague at that time are associated with the crowning glory of High Baroque architecture in the city: grand palaces and houses with bold façades, eye-catching pediments, portals, stucco and sculptural decoration that speak for the successful marriage of the arts as architects, sculptors, painters and craftsmen transformed the Lesser Quarter. Towards the end of the eighteenth century a more refined, decorative approach was favoured. Façades acquired the delicate Rococo stucco scrolls that still grace many a façade, some of them carefully picked out in pinks, greys and creams, others genteelly faded. The work was not confined to buildings: steep terraced gardens beneath the Castle and on Petřín Hill were included in the schemes. The frenzy of activity turned Prague into a major centre for the arts: Church and aristocracy kept countless goldsmiths, sculptors, designers and

others busy on the lavish interiors and grand exteriors of the new and renewed buildings.

Giovanni Santini Aichel (1667–1723) was the son and grandson of masons, whose father had often worked with Jean-Baptiste Mathey. As Santini was disabled, it was originally planned that he should become a painter rather than following the family tradition; little is known about his work in that field. In 1705, after travels in Austria and Italy, he settled in Valkoun House on Nerudova Street. He is described in the Lesser Quarter records as 'Mahler [Painter] und Architectus'. Most of his work was commissioned outside Prague as he was heavily involved in the restoration and rebuilding of major monasteries in the wave of activity that accompanied the re-Catholicization of Bohemia. For his revival of Gothic forms in his work for the Cistercians, Benedictines and Premonstratensians he has been called the Bohemian Hawksmoor.

However, Santini did not work exclusively for the monasteries. He had over forty secular patrons in 1722 and had some commissions in Prague, including three on the street where he lived. He was involved in the design of the Theatine church (Kostel Panny Marie ustavičné pomoci u kajetánů) with Jean-Baptiste Mathey, who gave the façade its restraint and classical austerity. The palaces for which Santini designed the façades, Morzin Palace (1714) and Thun-Hohenstein Palace (1716–26), both derive much of their effect from the incorporation of statues into the over-all design. In Prague, Santini worked with the two great Baroque sculptors, Ferdinand Maximilian Brokoff (1688–1731) and Matthias Bernard Braun (1684–1738). The Moors straining to uphold the Morzin balcony and the huge eagles curving around the doorway to the Thun-Hohenstein Palace reveal the monumentality and dynamism of their respective styles.

The Viennese architect Johann Bernhardt Fischer von Erlach (1656–1723) rebuilt the Old Town Clam-Gallas Palace from 1713. The massive portals and accented windows, doors and balconies may well have inspired Santini, whose façades show equal tension between classical sobriety and High Baroque flourishes. Von Erlach's work certainly influenced Giovanni Battista Alliprandi's plans for Lobkowic Palace (1703–7). Alliprandi (c. 1665–1720) worked in Vienna until 1697 and his Prague buildings are interpretations of Viennese Baroque style. The original plans for the palace draw on Fischer von Erlach's published design for a pleasure-garden house (Lustgartengebäude). Its most striking feature is the curve of the central pavilion projecting into the rear garden, complete with an ornamental pond on the roof. A gateway leads from the grand courtyard into an English-style park. The façade of Kaiserstein Palace on the Lesser Quarter Square is also Alliprandi's: this is a town house, without the grand setting of Lobkowic Palace, but it has retained its appearance from 1700, including the attic statues of the four seasons.

Like Lobkowic Palace, Schönborn Palace has an extensive garden on the slopes of Petřín Hill. It still has the carved gateway designed by Lurago but the façades were altered after 1715 by Guiseppe Bartolomeo Scotti (1684–1737) when the Braun workshop also designed statues of giants for the interior. The garden, with its little pavilion, can be glimpsed from the Castle Ramp: neither palace nor grounds are open to the public as the building now houses the American Embassy. Most of the Lesser Quarter palaces are now embassies or government offices and much of the town has to be admired from the outside or from above, staring down at the tiled roofs, gables, dormer windows and gardens of the residences lining the streets between Hradčany and the river. Whereas the interiors have been modified to suit the purposes of modern administration, the external appearance of the town, from the Castle, Strahov Monastery or Úvoz Street has not changed significantly since 1800.

There is a curious uniformity to accounts of life in these palaces from the eighteenth century onwards. As early as 1716 Lady Mary Wortley Montagu wrote to her sister about the town in tones demonstrating that in her view Prague played second fiddle to Vienna:

> . . . Those people of Quality who can-not easily bear the Expence of Vienna chuse to reside here, where they have assemblys, Music, and all other diversions (those of a Court excepted) at very moderate rates, all things being here in great Abundance, expecially the best wild fowl I ever tasted. I have allready been visited by some of the most considerable Ladys whose Relations I knew at Vienna. They are dress'd after the Fashions there, as people at Exeter imitate those of London.
>
> *(Complete Letters of Lady Mary Wortley Montagu,*
> 17 November 1716)

The families with palaces here also had country estates and, in some

Left above & below Kampa Island in the Vltava can be reached via the Lesser Quarter Charles Bridge. There were no houses here until the sixteenth century and the southern part of the island has remained a park to this day. The area to the north of the bridge is known as the 'Venice of Prague' as the houses lining a branch of the Vltava, the Certovka, are reminiscent of the *Serenissima;* like Venice, the island has some conservation problems.

Overleaf In 1357, Charles IV laid the foundation stone for the new bridge between the Old Town and the Lesser Quarter, designed by Peter Parler to replace the twelfth-century Judith Bridge, which had been destroyed by flooding. The fortified bridge was completed in the fifteenth century. It measures 520 × 10 metres and rests on sixteen arches. It was much praised at the time as an impressive feat of engineering; since the early eighteenth century it has been admired as an 'avenue of statues'. Many of the thirty religious works are from the workshops of the great Baroque sculptors of Prague, Matthias Bernard Braun and the Brokoff brothers.

cases, residences in Vienna. Generally they spent the winter in Prague, which was when diversions were most plentiful. Dr Charles Burney, travelling on the Continent in connection with his *General History of Music*, was in Prague in September 1772. The nobility was out of town, but he had been told that during the winter they had concerts in their palaces, often performed by their domestic staff, who learned to play at their country schools. Visitors in the nineteenth century also refer to the itinerant life-style of the aristocracy.

This was still their practice when Prince Alfons Clary was a student in the 1910s. He recalls in his memoirs that many palaces were empty as their owners were either on their country estates or in Vienna, but that they were open in the winter, and the setting for splendid balls during Carnival. His account of life in Prague includes glimpses of family heirlooms: Lobkowic pieces of inlaid furniture brought out of storage, the tapestries hung from the windows of Waldstein Palace as party decorations. In 1937 the Waldstein family put the palace at his disposal for a bazaar to raise money for children in the largely German-speaking Sudetenlands that had been hit by a serious economic depression. Clary's account of the occasion, which brought together members of the Kinsky, Buquoy, Clam-Gallas and Černín families, reads like the swan-song of the German-speaking, Vienna-oriented aristocracy, whose accommodations with Czechoslovakia came to an end by 1945: 'It took place in the garden of the Waldstein Palace, where the great Wallenstein had once resided and where the family was still living, where his stuffed horse was still to be seen, as well as the room from which [the astrologer] Seni had observed the stars.'

It is possible to visit some of these palaces either to hear concerts or see exhibitions like the Comenius Museum at Waldstein Palace or the collection of musical instruments at the Grand Prior's Palace (Palác maltézského velkopřevora). In the summer months many gardens are open to the public. The Italianate, terraced Ledebour, Pálffy, Černín and Fürstenberg gardens on the slope below the Castle are a striking extension of palaces on Waldstein Street. There were vineyards on the southern slope of Hradčany in the Middle Ages; they were transformed into gardens by those who settled there from the sixteenth century onwards. The *sala terrenas*, loggias, frescoes, staircases and fountains all date back to the eighteenth century. Ignác Palliardi (1737–1824), who planned the Rococo reconstruction of Kolowrat and Ledebour palaces, also had a hand in the planning of the gardens. The Vrtaba Gardens on Karmelitská Street are among the most celebrated: Santini's pupil František Maximilian Kaňka (1674–1766) designed the steep terraces on Petřín Hill, rising from a *sala terrena* with mythological paintings to a decorated observation area overlooking the Castle and Lesser Quarter. The sculpture in the gardens is from the workshop of Matthias Bernard Braun.

Along with Braun, Ferdinand Maximilian Brokoff and his brother Michael Joseph (1686–1721) produced most of the Baroque sculptures on the most celebrated outdoor work in Prague, the 'avenue of statues' on Charles Bridge. The eighteenth-century procession of saints brings an emotional charge to the bridge which was designed by Peter Parler for Charles IV, enhancing its ceremonial and decorative functions. From the outset, the bridge was many things: a link between settlements, a trade route, a set of coronation arches and a vital part of the defences of Prague. Sculptural decoration was a long-standing tradition: the west side of the Old Town Bridge Tower (Staroměstská mostecká věž) was very badly damaged during fighting with the Swedish army in 1648 but the east side still has its Gothic statues of St Adalbert, St Sigismund and St Vitus with Charles IV and Wenceslas IV (1378–1419).

There has been a crucifix on the bridge since the fourteenth century: in 1619, King Frederick's zealous Calvinist chaplain had it removed, along with other offensive graven images and statues in the towns. The citizens of Prague were adamant that it should be put back. The current bronze crucifix dating from 1629 bears a Hebrew inscription, placed there in 1695 by a Jew as punishment for blasphemy. The 1683 statue of St John of Nepomuk is the oldest one on the bridge. It stands at the very spot where according to legend he was hurled into the river by Wenceslas IV for refusing to reveal what the Queen had said during confession. St John was much venerated in re-Catholicized Bohemia: the Old Traveller reporting on his visit to Prague in 1857 noted that on St John's Day, 16 May, Prague was full of pilgrims. Beribboned shrines decorated with coloured lamps were put up all over the city, including one over the statue on the bridge: 'not for one moment did the Five Stars on the parapet remain untouched by the lips of devotees'.

It seems fitting that High Baroque Prague with its taste for evocative and decorative statuary should have added to the decoration of the

Far left The Old Town Bridge Tower was designed by Peter Parler and completed in 1391. Its western façade was damaged during fighting against the Swedish army in 1648 but the eastern one still bears its medieval sculptures. This detail shows the statues of St Adalbert and St Sigismund, patron saints of Bohemia.

Left There has been a cross on Charles Bridge since 1360. The present Calvary dates back to the seventeenth century. A Jew accused of blasphemy was ordered to pay for the inscription on the crucifix.

bridge, particularly with a series of appeals to faith that constitute a visual link between the church towers of the Old Town and those of the Lesser Quarter. Other statues were added in the nineteenth century, and the most recent one, St Cyril and St Methodius, in 1938. The sandstone has blackened over the years and some statues have been replaced by copies. In any case it is fair to say that it is in their over-all effect rather than as individual works of art that these sculptures are striking. They are especially effective seen from the other bridges in solemn procession across the river or as a companionable backdrop to the pedestrians, hawkers, guitarists and hangers-on who add to the sense of Charles Bridge as a place to go rather than a link between towns.

3 The Old Town (Staré Město)

On the West side of *Molda* [Vltava], is the Emperor's Castle, seated on a most high mountain, in the fall whereof is the Suburbe called *Kleinseit*, or little side. From this side to goe into the City, a long stone bridge is to be passed over *Molda*, which runs from the South to the North, and divides the suburbe from the City, to which as you goe, on the left side is a little City of the Jewes, compassed with walls, and before your eyes to the East, is the City called new *Prage*, both which Cities are compassed about with a third, called old *Prage*.

Itinerary, Fynes Moryson (1617)

Left The Renaissance façade of At the Minute House: this detail shows a seventeenth-century sgraffito figure and an eighteenth-century stone lion – from the days when the building was a pharmacy, At the White Lion.

Overleaf above The Old Town Hall was damaged by the Nazis during the Prague Rising of 8 May 1945. The Neo-Gothic wing was destroyed but the older parts of the building were not too badly affected and have since been restored. The burghers were granted the right to their own Town Hall in 1338, which was when they bought and rebuilt the corner house belonging to Wolflin of Kámen, adding the tower and its first-floor chapel. The entrance to Wolflin's house and the Renaissance window next to it, bearing the inscription 'Prague Caput Regni', date back to 1470–1520. The last two buildings in the block were substantially altered in the nineteenth century.

Overleaf below The Old Town Square seen from the Town Hall tower.

When the four towns of Prague were united in 1784, the Old Town Hall (Staroměstská radnice) became the seat of municipal government. The Town Hall Tower in the Old Town Square (Staroměstské náměstí) is one of the most popular sights in Prague. There is always a group of people standing in front of the fifteenth-century astronomical clock in anticipation of its hourly procession of the twelve apostles. This is tourist Prague *par excellence*: the houses along Celetná Street leading into the square boast bright new façades in shades of ochre, pink and green. With others on the Royal Way, they were scheduled for restoration relatively early on when work was resumed in the never-ending quest to preserve historic Prague. That was in 1964 after masonry brought down in torrential rains killed two pedestrians. Critics say that the façades are just that, a front behind which the fabric of the buildings is in serious need of attention. Others are disappointed that urban conservation here, as in other cities, means that expensive shops and restaurants catering to outside visitors have replaced the family homes and establishments that were there before. The slightly artificial bustle to the area today is a far cry from the daily routines of the musty pre-war neighbourhood with its smells of roast coffee, beer and smoked herring. The arguments are complicated ones, but the grim tower blocks in the modern districts of Prague – as well as other parts of the historic centre – stand in stark contrast to the area around the Old Town Square.

The Town Hall itself has a complicated history, involving purchases, conversions, building and restoration – most recently after it was

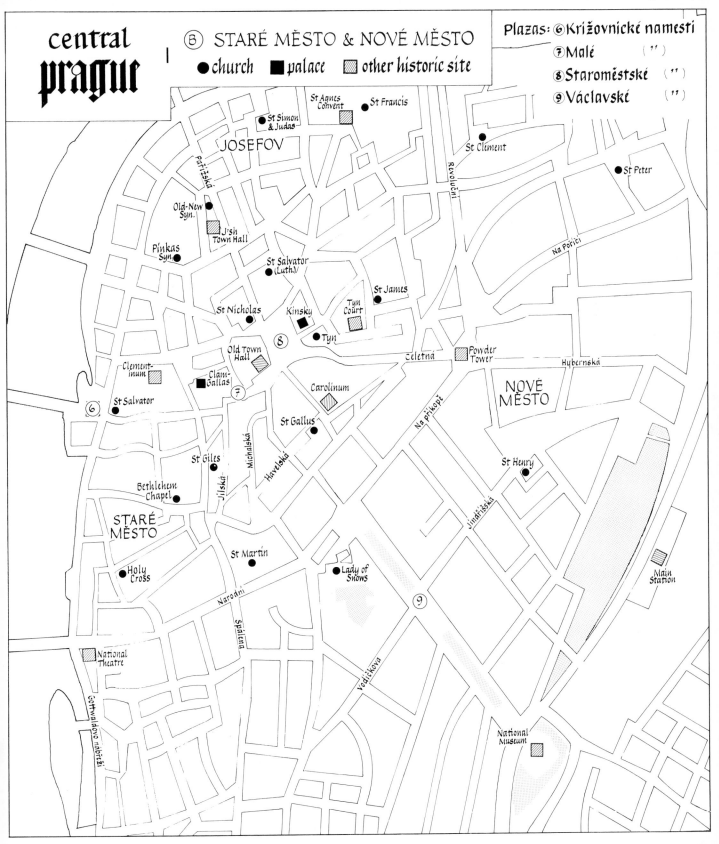

central prague

Ⓑ STARÉ MĚSTO & NOVÉ MĚSTO

● church ■ palace ▨ other historic site

Plazas: ⑥ Křižovnické namesti
⑦ Malé   (")
⑧ Staroměstské (")
⑨ Václavské   (")

JOSEFOV

St Agnes Convent
St Francis
St Simon & Judas
St Clement
St Peter

Pařížská

Old-New Syn.
J'sh Town Hall
Pinkas Syn.

St Salvator (Luth.)

Revoluční

Na Poříčí

St Nicholas
Kinsky
St Salvator
Tyn Court
St James

⑧ Tyn

Clementinum
Old Town Hall
Clam-Gallas
⑦
Carolinum
Powder Tower
Celetná
Hybernská

⑥ St Salvator

NOVÉ MĚSTO

St Gallus

Na příkopě

St Giles

Michalská
Havelská
Jilská

Bethlehem Chapel

St Henry

STARÉ MĚSTO

Jindřišská

St Martin

Holy Cross

Lady of Snows

Narodni

⑨

Spálena

Vodičkova

National Theatre

Main Station

Gottwaldovo nabřeží

National Museum

seriously damaged, and its neo-Gothic wing destroyed, by the Nazis at the close of the Second World War. It came about, however, for the simple reason that the thriving community that had grown up around the market square from the eleventh century onwards warranted this final confirmation of autonomous political status, granted to it by John of Luxemburg (1310–46) in 1338.

The Old Town of Prague was a trading town. The right bank of the Vltava attracted merchants and settlers at it was at the crossroads of the link between the two royal castles and long-distance trade routes: caravans crossing Europe forded the river at a point between the present Charles and Mánes bridges. One of the earliest descriptions of Prague is that of the tenth-century Jewish merchant Ibrahim Ibn Saud, who wrote admiringly of stone buildings and the market with its lively trade in poultry, grain, tin, furs, saddles – and slaves. From the eleventh century merchants had access not only to a large market place – the Old Town Square – but also the accommodation and storage facilities of the Týn Court, or Ungelt, where for a fee they enjoyed royal protection for the length of their stay. The tradition continued down the ages. The handsome Renaissance building, Granovský Palace, was built in 1560 to house visiting traders. It has an open loggia on the first floor with mythological and biblical wall paintings. The whole Court is now being restored and converted into hotels for the twentieth-century version of those travellers from afar.

The Přemyslids also extended royal protection to those who settled in Bohemia. Merchants and artisans were encouraged to come to Central and Eastern Europe as a spur to trade and manufacturing, and a counterweight to the nobility. There were two Jewish communities near the Old Town Square in the eleventh century with their own religious and administrative arrangements, as well as a French settlement around the Little Square (Malé náměstí) and a number of German colonies. Clusters of houses were built around churches – of which only one survives in its Romanesque form, the Rotunda of the Holy Cross (Rotunda sv Kříže). The tiny chapel nestling behind its neo-Romanesque iron grille was threatened with demolition in the nineteenth century and rescued by the Czech Artists' Union which oversaw its renovation. It is the only one in the Old Town, of the more than twenty estimated to have served the growing congregations in the area.

By the twelfth century there was a stone bridge over the river, Judith Bridge, the predecessor of Charles Bridge. The area between the market and the river came to be the most heavily populated. Some time around 1230 the built-up area with its stone houses, churches and monasteries was fortified and declared a royal town: the Old Town of Prague had asserted its primary role in the economy of the kingdom.

Wenceslas I (1230–53) granted land in the Old Town to a number of religious orders: the Minorites, Templars and Knights of the Cross settled in the newly fortified town during his reign. Many of the early monasteries were rebuilt, demolished or allowed to fall into disrepair as doctrine, taste and priorities changed over the centuries, culminating in the 1782 dissolution. The painstakingly restored Convent of St Agnes (Klášter Anežský) is therefore a valuable record of the transition to Gothic architecture in Prague, as well as an example of sensitive contemporary use of a historic monument: the cloisters and the churches of St Francis (Kostel sv Františka) and St Salvator (Kostel sv Salvátora) have been restored for use as an exhibition space and concert hall.

Thus by the time the burghers of the Old Town purchased the Early Gothic house belonging to Wolflin of Kámen on the market square and began to convert it into their Town Hall, the scattered settlements on the right bank had coalesced into a fortified town. We have some idea of what the thirteenth-century town looked like because over seventy Romanesque buildings have partially survived. Flooding of the type that destroyed Judith Bridge was such a problem that at the end of the thirteenth century it was decided to use landfill to build up the ground level by up to three metres. The first floors of some Romanesque and Early Gothic houses therefore became the cellars of their successors. These medieval rooms are now a feature of many Old Town bars and restaurants. In addition to admiring the vaulted cellars of establishments like U Sixtu on Celetná Street, it is possible to visit 'U Čapků' House, now a museum, where the cellar is in fact the entire first floor of a twelfth-century home.

There are further traces of the medieval town. The streets around the Church of St Gallus (Kostel sv Havla) date back to the thirteenth century. The medieval ground plan is evocative of the beginnings of the Old Town, of which some architectural signs remain. In what can be described as architectural pentimento, there is a house on Havelská

There has been an astronomical clock on the south face of the Old Town Hall tower since 1410. It is made up of three parts: the most recent is the Joseph Mánes calendar of 1866 with its inner circle of the signs of the Zodiac and outer one of scenes from rural life representing the months of the year. Above the calendar, the clock face shows the time and the movements of the Sun and Moon – around the Earth, according to the fifteenth-century world-view. When the hour strikes, the twelve Apostles, preceded by the Devil bearing an hourglass, parade past the little windows in the upper portion of the clock.

Street where a Gothic arch is embedded in the later façade. The House at the Iron Door (Dům U železných dveří) has a Gothic entrance on Michalská Street and a Renaissance one on Jilská Street. In the Old Town there is a sense of architectural continuity stretching back to the twelfth century. Remarkably, an entire Gothic building recently emerged unscathed from underneath a Baroque one. The House at the Stone Bell (Dům U kamenného zvonu) on the Old Town Square was scheduled for demolition until it was realized that the eighteenth-century façade concealed a fourteenth-century palace, probably belonging to John of Luxemburg.

The citizens engaged in building their Town Hall Tower after 1338 would have had no reason to suspect the momentous changes in the years ahead. With the accession of Charles IV to the thrones of Bohemia and the Holy Roman Empire the Old Town of Prague entered a new phase. Prague became an imperial city, with a population of 40 000 and great cultural renown. While the major building projects of Charles IV involved the Castle and the New Town, his Golden Age came to the Old Town, too. It was here he founded his University, the Carolinum. Emperor and Pope determined the statutes of the institution which was to train jurists and clergymen to serve the Holy Roman Empire. The Paris model of organization was followed, and members of the University divided into Saxon, Bavarian, Polish and Czech 'nations' for administrative purposes. Initially a reflection of the cosmopolitan nature of one of the biggest cities in Europe, ranked with the universities of Bologna, Paris and Oxford, the Carolinum became the seat of debates that were one strand in the development of that very Bohemian phenomenon, Hussitism.

No individual building was allocated to the Carolinum originally. It was only in 1383 that Wenceslas IV made Rothlow House available: the Gothic foundations and arches remain, as well as the remarkable oriel window that has become the symbol of the University. By the time the scholars had been given this building voices were being raised in Prague against alleged corruption, laxity and opulence in the Church. In a bitter debate complicated by considerations of political expediency and nationality, the Czech 'nation' of the Carolinum spearheaded the campaign in support of the theses of the Englishman John Wyclif (c.1330–84). Giving theological expression to popular anti-clericalism and demands for vernacular preaching, the Bohemian members of the

The Rotunda of the Holy Cross is one of the oldest surviving Romanesque buildings in Prague. It was threatened with demolition in the nineteenth century, but rescued and renovated by the Czech Artists' Union.

Above At the Two Golden Bears on Kožná Street has a charming Renaissance portal.

Below The monument to John Huss by Ladislav Šaloun was placed in the centre of the Old Town Square on 6 July 1915, five hundred years after the reformer had been burned at the stake.

University were inspired by the teachings of men like Conrad of Waldhausen (d.1369) and Milíč of Kroměříž (d.1374) to argue for Church reform. When the reformer John Huss (1371–1415) was made rector of the Carolinum and complaints of the Czech 'nation' against the domination of the Germans were given a sympathetic hearing by Wenceslas IV, two thousand German scholars and students decamped to Leipzig, leaving behind a foundation that was to become a centre of heresy in the eyes of the Church.

Huss enjoyed the support of Wenceslas IV for a few more years, but he had to flee in 1412 after his condemnation of the papal sale of indulgences led to his excommunication. In 1414 he agreed to appear before the Constance Council: the safe conduct granted by Emperor Sigismund notwithstanding, Huss was condemned as a heretic and burned at the stake on 7 June 1415. His death gave rise to a movement that united the very disparate groups advocating Church reform for reasons running from questions of faith, to resentment of German control of town economies, to eagerness to acquire Church property. During the fifteenth century the Old Town was the centre of what emerged as the moderate faction in a complex network of interests: the Carolinum, the Town Hall and a number of churches were at the heart of a movement that shaped Bohemian culture until 1620 and inspired the National Revival that began at the end of the eighteenth century.

Huss preached at Bethlehem Chapel (Betlémská kaple) from 1402 until he had to flee Prague. In the eighteenth century the chapel was demolished but for three outer walls: the building that stands in Bethlehem Square (Betlémské náměsti) today is the result of extensive restoration carried out in the 1950s. The plain chapel stands in stark contrast to Baroque Prague and seems to embody Hussite strictures against the worldliness of the Church. The accommodation provided for the preacher was a converted malt house, which seems entirely apposite for the man who included in the sins of priests their extravagant and unnecessary building projects. The chapel could hold three thousand people, and the sermons in Czech addressing popular grievances against the Church made it the centre of the movement early on.

Jakoubek of Stribo (1372–1429) was one of the most influential of those scholars who continued Huss's campaign for Church reform. He was responsible for instituting the practice of communion in both kinds (*sub utraque specie*) which no longer restricted communion wine to the officiating priest. It was this practice that led to the Hussites being called Utraquists. This was done for the first time in October 1414, in a little Romanesque church that had been rebuilt after 1350 when the nave was raised and the tower added on. St-Martin-in-the-Wall (Kostel sv Martina ve zdi) was originally the church of a community called Újezd. When the settlement was cut in two by the Old Town fortifications, the church was included in the town – hence the name.

Týn Church has long symbolized the Old Town; its sturdy towers and picturesque turrets rising behind the graceful arcades of the Venetian-style Týn School have inspired a number of writers, no one more lyrical than the Victorian Old Traveller:

> Small turrets rise from the angles of the towers; each of the latter has a spire composed of eight planes, in its centre, and from four out of the eight, spring slender spiral shafts: the numerous points, presented by all, are profusely adorned with glittering balls, crosses, and stars of gilded iron, gleaming brightly in the sunshine, which here, and at this season, rarely fails to add its life-giving touch to the landscape.

It too was a Hussite church. The original building was part of the Týn Court; construction of the present church dates back to the beginning of the reign of Charles IV, and the beautiful tympanum of the north portal (now in the National Gallery) comes from the Peter Parler workshop. While the church was not completed until the early sixteenth century, it was the main town church during the Hussite period; Waldhauser and Milíč of Kroměříž both preached there, as did John of Rokycana (d.1471), the Hussite archbishop. During the reign of the last native King of Bohemia, George of Poděbrady (1458–71), both his statue and a gold chalice adorned the west gable that he had completed; in 1626 the statue had to make way for one of the Madonna, and it is said that the chalice was melted down to make her halo.

The significance of the chalice was well understood by visitors to Prague. Fynes Moryson reported that: 'Upon the outsyde of the dore of the Cathedrall Church in the cheefe Citty of Prague they have ingraven a sworde and a Challice, in memory that by the sworde they extorted from the Pope liberty to Communicate as well the Cupp or blood as the body of our lord in the holy Eucharist.' The reference to violence is

Matěj Rejsek began work on the Powder Tower in 1475 when the court was still in residence nearby. The Late Gothic tower lost much of its significance after Vladislav Jagiello moved the court back to Hradčany in 1484. It was not actually finished until 1886, when it acquired its Neo-Gothic gallery and roof and the statues of Bohemian kings and saints that complement the fifteenth-century decorative scheme.

entirely apposite: the first half of the fifteenth century in Bohemia was marked by warfare, of which Prague had its share. Wenceslas IV died in 1419 and the Estates could not accept that Sigismund inherit the throne. Utraquism became the rallying call of those opposed to the rule of the man responsible for Huss's death. He led no fewer than five crusades against them, to no avail. During the 1420 siege of Prague, he did take Hradčany and Vyšehrad castles, but was repulsed from the right bank by John Žižca (*c.*1360–1424), the great Hussite military leader. In 1436 the Council of Basle negotiated the Compacts, creating the conditions whereby Sigismund could claim his throne. He returned to Prague that year and died in 1437. Even before the truce, however, the Hussites were split between the radical Taborites and the Utraquists who were prepared to come to some accommodation with the Church and Crown. The moderates won the fratricidal battle of Lipany on 30 May 1434: the multiplicity of interests involved could no longer be contained within one movement. Not until the election of George of Poděbrady in 1458 did some kind of peace return to Prague.

The Hussites are of key importance to the history of the Reformation as they prefigured sixteenth-century Protestantism. The movement came to have a different significance to the Czechs, for whom John Huss became a symbol of national resistance. The fact that his followers successfully resisted the five crusades led against them was of central importance to people who had been crushed at the Battle of White Mountain. The historian and politician František Palacký (1798–1876) compared the Hussite period favourably with the 'era of darkness' after 1620. Tomas Garrigue Masaryk (1850–1937), the first president of the Republic of Czechoslovakia, lectured on Huss in Geneva in 1915 at the outset of his campaign for an independent Czechoslovak republic; in the same year a monument was raised to him in the Old Town Square. Nor has Huss been the preserve of Czech democrats: it was the Communist government of Klement Gottwald that decided to rebuild Bethlehem Chapel in 1950, claiming that it demonstrated the ancient pedigree of Bohemian communism.

The century following the reign of Charles IV was therefore one of upheaval, marked more by destruction than construction. Even before Wenceslas IV had to contend with political strife in Bohemia and the Empire he betrayed little of his father's taste for grand architectural schemes: short of completing the Old Town Bridge Tower, he did little to change the appearance of the Prague towns. The social unrest that characterized the latter part of his reign destabilized the former pride of Empire. Many buildings were destroyed in the riots and battles of the 1420s; Hussite iconoclasm and wrath were vented on the monasteries, many of which were deserted during that time. St Agnes was badly damaged, as were a number of Lesser Quarter monasteries. The situation improved after the election of George of Poděbrady; he and his successor, Vladislav Jagiello, actually embarked on building projects.

It should be borne in mind, however, that this was a century of considerable importance to the Old Town; it was a matter of some prestige that the court was based there from the reign of Wenceslas IV until 1484, when Vladislav Jagiello moved back to Hradčany. Nothing but a commemorative plaque attests to that fact: political power of a different stripe was enshrined in the Municipal House (Obecní dům) built on the site in the early twentieth century. The one extant construction associated with the court in the Old Town is the Powder Tower (Prašná brána). It stands on the site of an earlier gateway and was begun by Vladislav Jagiello before he moved the court away from the Old Town. The Tower – echoing the Bridge Tower, and attributed an equally ceremonial role – was left unfinished until the late nineteenth century, when it acquired its present roof and gallery. It had been used as a storehouse for gunpowder in the intervening years, which is how it got its name.

While the Old Town was home to the court, its own institutions acquired considerable influence during the Hussite years. The scholars at the Carolinum made up the Consistory responsible for running the Church, and the Town Hall took a number of initiatives, a tradition that did much to fuel burgher resentment of the Habsburgs' erosion of their prerogatives. While the town's political significance declined during the sixteenth century, economic recovery and religious tolerance provided some continuity with times past. It is testimony to the religious eclecticism commented on by visitors before 1620 that churches built at that time included the Italian Chapel (Vlašská kaple), the Jesuit Church of St Salvator on Knights of the Cross Square (Křižovnické náměstí), the Lutheran Church of St Salvator on Salvátorská Street, funded by contributions from throughout Protestant Europe and the Church of Saints Simon and Judas (Kostel sv Šimona a Judy) of the Bohemian Brethren.

Fynes Moryson exclaimed about the religious variety that had masters and servants attending different churches:

> Generally in all the kingdome there was great confusion of Religions, so as in the same Citty some were Calvinists, some Lutherans, some Hussites, some Anabaptists, some Picards, some Papists, not only in the Cheefe Citty Prage, and the other Cittyes of Bohemia, as Bodly and Spill, but in Sperona and Graniza Cittyes of Moravia. And as the Jews have a peculyar Citty at Prage, so they had freedome throughout all the kingdom.

The Jewish community was of course a part of that landscape – and yet not: the 'peculyar Citty' was indeed a separate town, a settlement dating back to the twelfth century, when the Jews, like other migrants, settled in the vicinity of the market place. Any inclination they might have had to stick together would have been reinforced by the injunction of the Third Lateran Council that Jews and Christians should live separately. The Jews of Prague were therefore confined to their quarters within the Old Town, a walled community with four gates that afforded minimal protection against the outside world. They too clustered around their temple: after Přemysl Otaker II reconfirmed their status as direct royal subjects, the community was granted permission to build a synagogue. The Old-New Synagogue (Staronová synagoga), probably built by the stonemasons at work on St Agnes Convent, is the oldest surviving building in the Jewish quarter and is still in use. Whereas other synagogues in the town came to be incorporated into other buildings, the Old-New Synagogue has always been free-standing, surrounded by an open space that served as a market place and provided some relief from the often cramped conditions.

Numbers fluctuated considerably in the town in the course of the sixteenth century: around 1500 there were often several families to a house as Jews fleeing worsening conditions in Germany sought better lives for themselves to the East; then the troubles migrated too: burghers intent on protecting their guilds and resentful of any Jewish involvement in trade or manufacturing brought pressure to bear on the Crown to expel them. In 1541, after the fire that was itself the source of great tension in Prague, all but fifteen families were banished. While they were able to return a few years later, the threat of pogroms and exile hung over the community, able to protect itself only in so far as its

The Old Jewish Cemetery served as a burial ground from the first half of the fifteenth century until 1787. As space was limited, the community developed the practice of burying older graves under fresh earth brought in to accommodate new ones. The crowded cemetery, with its uneven terrain and jumble of tombstones, is an arresting sight.

Overleaf left Most of the Jewish quarter of Prague was razed during slum clearances at the end of the nineteenth century. The early Gothic Old-New Synagogue is the oldest of the six synagogues that were left standing and the only one still in use; it was built after the Jews of Prague were granted the status of royal subjects in 1254. The double-naved synagogue with its distinctive high saddle roof and gables was probably built by stonemasons working on nearby St Agnes Convent.

Overleaf right Maisel Synagogue now houses the silver collection of the State Jewish Museum. It was built by Burgomaster Mordecai Maisel, at the end of the sixteenth century. It burned down in 1689, was repaired shortly afterwards and rebuilt in Neo-Gothic style at the end of the nineteenth century.

Most of the buildings in Josefov, as the Jewish town was known from 1850, were demolished at the end of the nineteenth century. They were replaced by apartment blocks like this one on Pařížská Street with its characteristically exuberant façade. These Art Nouveau buildings have been neglected, poorly restored or unsympathetically modernized. It is only relatively recently that their importance to the architectural heritage of Prague has been recognized.

money-lending activities were indispensable to the sovereign and the aristocracy.

The Jewish community depended heavily on the goodwill of the Crown. The elders who governed the town and mediated between Jews and court were royal appointees, and the King had to approve the Chief Rabbi chosen by the congregation. These officials were chosen from among the wealthiest members of the community, as they were in the best position to defend their fellow Jews and meet the exactions of the King. The successful members of the community were also behind the building activities in the town, which included some ambitious projects despite the lack of space. The architectural patrons of the sixteenth century – the period referred to as the Renaissance in the ghetto – included the very prominent Horowitz family, and the burgomaster Mordecai Maisel (1528–1601).

Pinkas Synagogue was financed by Zalman Horowitz, one of the wealthiest members of the family. It seems that the decision to build a family temple was taken in the light of community reluctance to recognize the family's royal privilege to have two members automatically made elders. The new synagogue was the headquarters of the Horowitz camp in a bitter dispute revealing that whatever the solidarity in the face of outside hostility, disparities in wealth and influence had their effects here as elsewhere. The synagogue combines Late Gothic elements – vaulting, buttresses and tracery windows – with the introduction of Renaissance motifs like the fluting on the buttresses and the entrance portal. It has been seriously damaged by flooding over the years and remodelled several times. It is currently being restored.

Burgomaster Maisel financed many building projects in the Jewish town. He built a hospital, a home for the poor and a school as well as paving the public areas of the town and financing the construction of the Town Hall and two more synagogues, which are still standing. The buildings bear little resemblance to their original form, however: Meisel Synagogue burned down in 1689. It was rebuilt on a smaller scale than the original and remodelled in the nineteenth century. The Town Hall and High Synagogue, which were built simultaneously in Renaissance style, were also altered in later years.

The reason for the extensive renovation of the synagogues at the end of the nineteenth century was that the whole area was subject to a vast slum clearance project: the crowded conditions of the ghetto had not

Left and above right Celetná Street leads from the Powder Tower to the Old Town Square. Many of the houses date back to the earliest days of the Old Town and have preserved Romanesque and Gothic masonry in their cellars. They were rebuilt over the centuries and present passers-by with a series of colourful and decorative Baroque façades.

Far right The turrets of Týn Church on the Old Town Square.

Below right Detail of the Renaissance ironwork on the fountain in the Little Square, which is located just off the Old Town Square.

improved, even after the Jews had been freed from restrictions by the reforms of the eighteenth and nineteenth centuries. All of the tenements were demolished: six synagogues, the Town Hall and the cemetery now stand in recollection of the thriving community that once lived there. Some who could afford to stay on in the apartment buildings that were put up at the beginning of the century did so; the others had to move to the outskirts of Prague. The exuberant sculptural and stucco decoration, ironwork, coloured inlays and mosaics of those buildings are all associated with Art Nouveau in Prague. There is even talk of 'Pařízská Street Style' as the parade of apartment buildings leading off from the Old Town Square provides a particularly rich example of architectural thinking at the time. Yet they have not always enjoyed this respect, and as a result have been either neglected or clumsily modernized. Now that they have an acknowledged place in the architectural heritage of the city, greater interest is being shown in their state of repair.

The later buildings do rather dwarf the remains of the ghetto, however. Perhaps the mild sense of claustrophobia is not unrelated to the sense of enclosure that the residents must have had at times. In the light of the fate of the residents of Prague's Jewish Town at the hands of the Nazis who deported and murdered 36 000 people, it seems somehow fitting that the Old Jewish Cemetry (Starý žlidovský hřbitov) is the place with the strongest associations with the Renaissance ghetto: Maisel is buried there, as is the astronomer and historian David Gans (1541–1613) and Rabbi Löw (1512–1609), the learned scholar who came to be associated with stories of the cabbala and magic in a trend that culminated in the nineteenth-century story of the Golem, the servant that he was said to have fashioned out of clay. Many, many others are buried there; the ornate sandstone and marble gravestones were crowded together as the Jews who lived apart had to be buried apart too.

The separate existence of the Jews in Prague is demonstrated by the community's attitude to the rebellion of 1618. Caught between the Estates and the Crown, the community kept a low profile, revealing its allegiance with a generous gift to Ferdinand II after the Battle of White Mountain. Just as later generations had to grapple with the identity problems raised by increasing tension between Czech and German speakers, the Jews in 1618 had to determine the best course to follow in an often hostile environment.

The defeat of White Mountain was brought home to the Old Town in no uncertain terms. A purportedly true – and chillingly clinical – account of the execution on 21 June 1621 of those behind the 1618 rebellion against Ferdinand II sets the scene for their bloody end:

> The Theatrum or Scaffold of timber which was to be erected, and whereupon the following Execution of the prisoners for the most part was to be performed, was made ready and dispatched in the common Carpenters yarde of the olde Citty; and the same was the next day erected and set up in the great Market-place of the said Cittie close and ioyning to the Towne-house, so that they might out of the same Town-house goe conviently upon the Scaffold through a dore purposely made to that end. The Scaffold being 4 ells: 22 paces broade, and 22 paces long, in a square forme: all of good substantial strong timber and rayles made round about.

It was the beginning of a new era. The religious eclecticism of the Old Town surrendered to Catholic hegemony. Just as in the Lesser Quarter, property changed hands, churches were remodelled and the Baroque made its grand entrance. It is interesting to consider the way in which some of the churches were 'Barocized': there was of course a whole range of solutions affecting exteriors and interiors. The Church of St Giles (Kostel sv Jiljí) from the outside looks to all extents and purposes like the Gothic building that it is: with an austere quality in keeping with a Hussite parish church. Little betrays the eighteenth-century interior commissioned by the Dominicans who had owned it since 1626: the frescoes and altars speak to an entirely different sensibility. The Church of St James (Kostel sv Jakuba) has one of the most beautiful interiors in the Old Town, heralded by some rather unconvincing stucco reliefs on the façade. In addition to its profusion of colour, the church boasts one of the best-known Baroque tombs, that designed by Fischer von Erlach for Count Vratislav Mitrovic. The Church of St Gallus was granted to the Carmelites who had the façade rebuilt in the eighteenth century: while the interior still has a number of Gothic touches, the undulating façade is entirely Baroque.

Jean-Baptiste Mathey's Church of St Francis (1679–88) was one of the first Baroque churches to be built in the Old Town. His patron, the Archbishop, had been Grand Master of the Knights of the Cross, which is how Mathey came to design their centrally planned, domed church on Knights of the Cross Square. The four arms of the church extend from the oval central space that rises into one of the first domes built in Prague.

The Jesuits had already come to the Old Town before 1620. Work continued on their Church of St Salvator under the direction of Carlo Lurago and Francesco Caratti; the portico and statues of church fathers, Jesuit saints, the evangelists, the Virgin and Christ were added in 1659: looking out over the Square of the Knights of the Cross, the statues add a curiously human touch to the façade. They seem to complete the effect of the 'avenue of statues' by beckoning those who have stepped off the Charles Bridge into the Church. The façade of St Salvator's and the curve of the Italian Chapel provide some relief from the sobriety of the Clementinum, the Jesuit College, of which they are a part. The huge complex is second only to the Castle in area, covering the space originally taken up by 25 houses, as well as a number of churches and gardens and a monastery property that the Order bought up gradually. Also designed by architects of the North Italian school, it is built around five courtyards, the buildings divided up into successions of single rooms joined by corridors. Building proceeded throughout the seventeenth and eighteenth centuries, and included another church, St Clement (Kostel sv Klimenta), as well as Kaňka's richly decorated Chapel of Mirrors, now an exhibition room and concert hall.

The Carolinum was joined to the Clementinum after White Mountain; the Jesuits played a central role in education in Prague as elsewhere, providing secondary and higher education in addition to the training of their novices. From 1654 the University was called the Charles-Ferdinand University, and the Carolinum itself was rebuilt from 1718 after a design by Kaňka. By the time the Jesuits were expelled from Bohemia in 1773, tensions in Prague society were centred more on language than faith. One of the ways in which Bohemian nationalists sought to defend themselves against the government reforms that had their lives run increasingly from Vienna – and in German – was to advocate linguistic parity for Czech. In the long term this led to the University being split in two, with the Czechs and Austrian-Germans going their separate ways in matters of education as in so much else.

The Old Town Square also changed during the Baroque Age. In

Above The Old Town Church of St Nicholas was built in 1732–5 after plans by Kilián Dientzenhofer. The long southern façade with the main entrance and towers was designed for the original cramped site: the buildings which closed the church off from the Old Town Square have since been demolished.

Below The interior of the Church of St Nicholas.

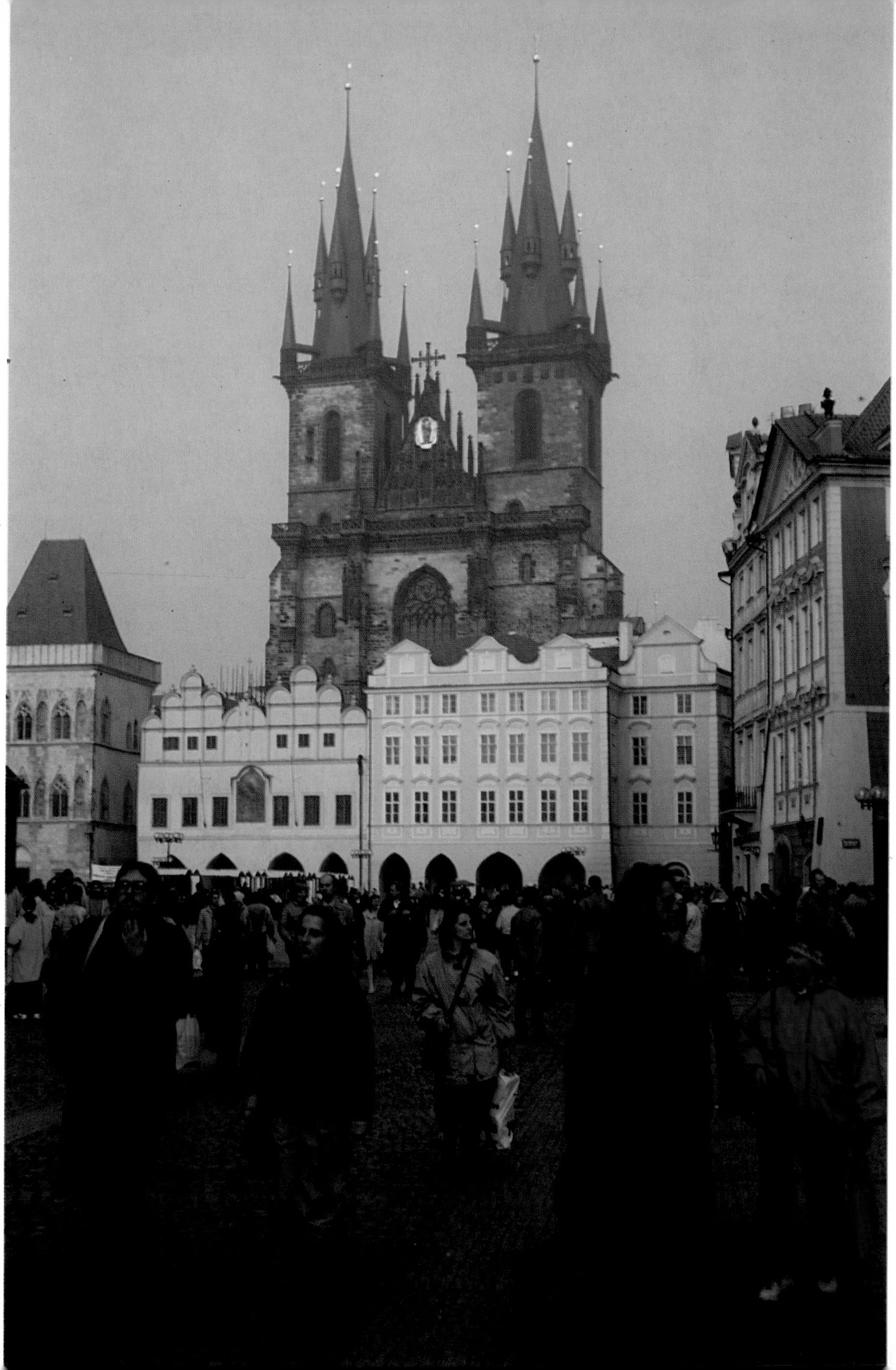

Left The towers of Týn Church rise 80 metres behind the Venetian-style gables of the Týn School and the Baroque façade of At the White Unicorn. Building on the church began in the mid-fourteenth century. The west gable dates back to the reign of the Hussite King George of Poděbrady; it originally bore a statue of the King and a golden chalice, the symbol of the Hussite movement. In 1626 they were replaced with a statue of the Virgin, the only Baroque touch to the resolutely Gothic exterior.

Above left The interior of Týn Church.

Above right The Church of St James was founded in 1232, rebuilt in the fourteenth century and later recast as a Baroque church. The sumptuous pink, cream and gold interior (1736–9) with its twenty-one altars and ceiling frescoes is one of the most successful instances of 'Barocization'.

The east side of the Old Town
Square with the fourteenth-
century façade of the House At
the Stone Bell and the Rococo
Goltz-Kinský Palace.

1635, the Benedictines were granted the Church of St Nicholas, where Hussite members of the University had once attended mass. The Order built a monastery and commissioned Kilián Dientzenhofer to build them a new church (1732–7). The site was a difficult one, as the church was hemmed in by conventual buildings that have since been demolished, which now gives it a rather ungainly appearance.

Across the square stands Goltz-Kinský Palace, which Dientzenhofer designed and Anselmo Lurago (1701–65) built for Count Goltz between 1755 and 1765. The attic statues and stucco decoration make it a classic Late Baroque palace. It now houses the National Gallery's collection of graphic art, but it has had a varied history, revealing once again the peculiar fate of these palaces for which their owners had minimal use. Prince Clary stayed there when he was a student in Prague, and reports his rooms had no bathroom or electricity, and that in addition to the Kinský family *pied-à-terre*, the palace boasted an entire German grammar school, a lawyer's office and some storage facilities for merchants.

It was from the balcony of the palace that Klement Gottwald addressed the Prague crowds after what the Communist government chose to call the February Victory of 1948. It was a gesture equating the masterminds of the 'bloodless coup' with Huss, whose brooding presence dominates the square, or the heroes of the Prague Rising against the Nazis. The magnificent sweep of the Old Town Square does indeed make a grand setting for gestures of that nature, though, as has been said many times, Gottwald and his successors had a selective memory – so much so that for his ruthless campaign to root out all evidence of the Prague Spring of 1968, Kundera called President Husák the 'president of forgetting'. Husák himself is just a memory now, part of the complicated history of Prague. Yet standing in Old Town Square and scrutinizing the buildings, there is ample opportunity to meditate on the passage of time in Prague and what took place there from the twelfth to the twentieth centuries. It would be rather ironic if the passing of the 'era of forgetting' led to Prague being overwhelmed by visitors and investors with scant regard for that heritage.

4 The New Town (Nové Město)

> As Charles the Fourth had resolved so he did. At once he set to work to make all the preparations for the founding of the new town. He himself defined its extent and the line of its ramparts, and himself laid the foundation for them. He was present at the measuring out of the streets, he decided the site of the market and the square. Often he talked and took counsel with the builder, and often came to see how the work was progressing, and on every occasion he spoke to a mason here or a day-labourer there, questioned them and made them gifts, pleased that the work was continuing successfully.
>
> *Legends of Old Bohemia*, Alois Jirásek (London, 1963)

P rague's New Town is a feat of medieval town-planning. While there was nothing unusual in the decision to relieve over-crowding in the fortified areas by founding a new community, the sheer size of Charles IV's undertaking is remarkable. The idea of a medieval town often conjures up visions of a picturesque, huddled, higgledy-piggledy settlement – not the wide streets, sweeping squares and meticulous arrangements of the New Town. The layout of the original town is still clear on contemporary maps: it curved around the Old Town fortifications that ran along present-day Revoluční, Na příkopě and Národní Streets. Stretching from Poříčí to Vyšehrad, its main axes – now known as Hybernská Street, Wenceslas Square (Václavské náměstí) and Charles Square (Karlovo náměstí) – prolonged the main roads of the Old Town, and were linked by Jindřišská and Vodičkova Streets. The dimensions of streets and markets were strictly regulated, as were building standards. Tax incentives were granted to those able to put up their houses to specification within a given period.

Early settlers included the Church: the parish churches of St Stephen (Kostel sv Štěpána) and St Henry (Kostel sv Jindřicha) provided focal points for the development of the upper and lower parts of town. Charles IV also invited a number of religious orders to come to his new town: the Augustinians, Servites and Benedictines were among those who built the churches, convents and monasteries there in the fourteenth century. Many of them suffered in the course of the Hussite Wars: from the outset the population of the New Town included

Elegant façades on the Gottwald Embankment.

The Šítek water tower once fed the fountains of the New Town. The 1495 building was rebuilt in 1591 and 1648 and acquired its Baroque dome in the eighteenth century. It got its name from the Šítka mills that used to stand on the Gottwald Embankment. The site is now occupied by the white Constructivist Mánes Building of 1930.

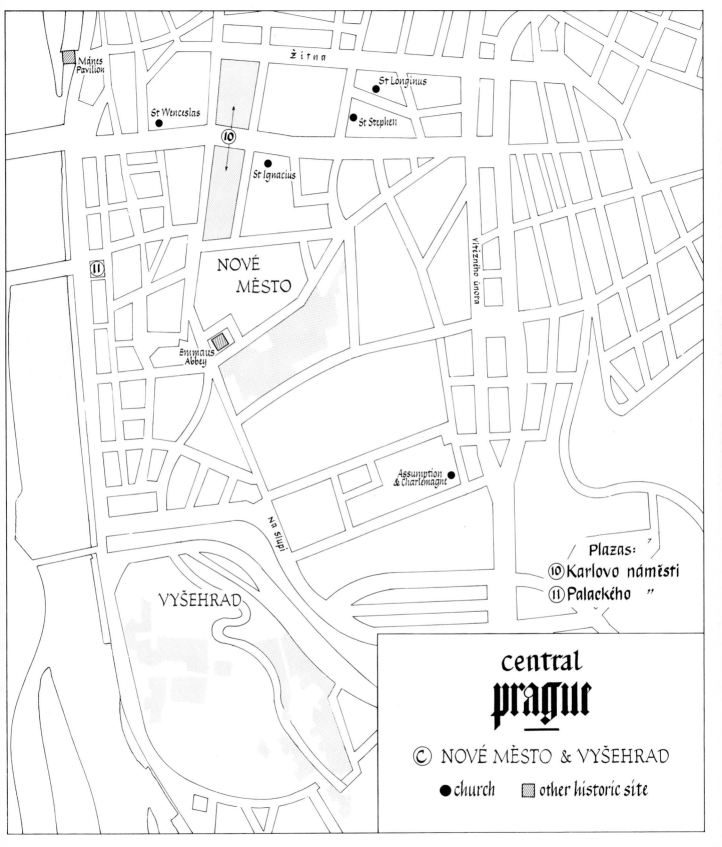

Žitna

Mánes
Pavilion

St Longinus

St Wenceslas

St Stephen

10

St Ignacius

11

NOVÉ
MĚSTO

Vítězného února

Emmaus
Abbey

Assumption
& Charlemagne

Na slupi

Plazas:

10 Karlovo náměstí

11 Palackého "

VYŠEHRAD

central

prague

© NOVÉ MĚSTO & VYŠEHRAD

● church   ▨ other historic site

poorer craftsmen, to whom the reformers' strictures against the worldliness of the Church had particular appeal.

Whatever the fury of the New Town residents, their destruction was often made good. Many of the early churches survive, if not in their original form, whereas the rest of the town was considerably rebuilt from the nineteenth century onwards. Thus the medieval town plan has had a modern city built on it. As a result, the New Town has much less of the immediate charm of the others, where the accumulation of towers, spires, gables and ornate façades are a constant feast for the eye. It is also the historic town to have suffered the most from neglect and ill-considered modern building projects: most notoriously the inner-ring road that blocks the Art Nouveau Main Station (Hlavní nádraží) of 1909 designed by Josef Fanta (1856–1954). That said, it is the centre of modern Prague and warrants a visit from those wanting to recapture Charles IV's town, get a sense of the city as a whole or explore the ways in which architects working in the nineteenth and twentieth centuries engaged with the past, with nationalism and with the requirements of modern urban development.

The New Town absorbed some earlier settlements and their churches, some of which survive. The twelfth-century Rotunda of St Longinus (Rotunda sv Longina) was the parish church of Rybníček and it was built at the same time as the Rotunda of the Holy Cross in the Old Town. It acquired its Baroque turret in the seventeenth century and was restored in 1844 after having been used as a warehouse. The Romanesque church of St Peter in Poříčí (Kostel sv Petra) was rebuilt once the former German merchant community became part of the New Town, as was the Zderaz church of St Wenceslas (Kostel sv Václava). Of the churches built during the reign of Charles IV, many bear the stamp of his ambitions: the Church of the Assumption of Our Lady and Charlemagne (Kostel Panny Marie a Karla Velikého) dedicated to his patron saint was modelled on the octagonal imperial burial church in Aachen; the octagonal nave was not vaulted until 1575. Our Lady of the Snows (Kostel Panny Marie Sněžné) was founded in connection with his coronation. It was intended to be grander still than St Vitus but only the choir was completed before financial problems and the Hussite Wars intervened. The area around the church has been built up and it is surprisingly easy when near it to miss the truncated grandeur clearly visible from, say, the Old Town Hall Tower.

Right The New Town was founded by Charles IV in 1348 and incorporated a number of earlier settlements. The tiny Romanesque Rotunda of St Longinus was the parish church of the community of Rybníček. It was used as a storehouse from 1782 until its rescue and restoration in the nineteenth century.

Far right The Benedictine Emmaus Monastery was very badly damaged in an American air raid at the close of the Second World War. The western façade of the church was restored in 1967. Its modern steeples are a striking addition to the spires of Prague but they are proving too heavy for the church, which has been sadly neglected otherwise.

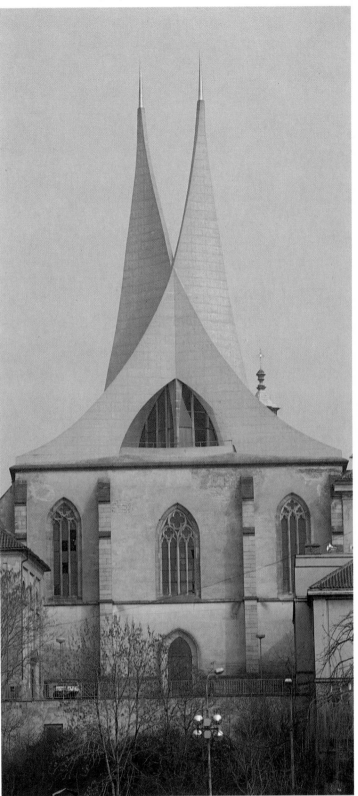

The wall paintings of 1360–70 in the cloister of Emmaus Monastery were restored in 1960. These scenes from the Old and New Testaments are important examples of Bohemian Gothic art.

Emmaus Abbey, or the Abbey of the Slavs (Klášter na Slovanech), was founded by Charles IV in 1347 for the Benedictines of the Slav rite. The abbey reflected the Church's interest in bringing populations to the south and east of Bohemia into the fold. In that connection, the monastery produced Slavonic manuscripts, notably the illuminated Emmaus Bible (1360), Czech translations of the Bible and the Rheims book of Gospels used for the coronation oath of French kings. Emmaus supported the Hussite movement, and was home to the Englishman, Peter Payne (c.1380–1455), who negotiated with such skill for the movement. The monastery was considerably altered by the Spanish and German Benedictines who lived there after 1635. However, the Gothic wall paintings in the original cloister were preserved; the scenes from the Old and New Testaments were restored in 1960, part of the attempt to repair the monastery which was severely damaged in an American air raid at the close of the Second World War.

After the War, it was decided to house some institutes of the Czechoslovak Academy of Sciences in the monastery, a decision that was rather at variance with its having been proclaimed a national cultural monument, because the heavy equipment used in some of the research carried out there was not sympathetic to the fabric of the building. Nor was the restoration work adequate: from the outside, the 1965 spires on the church are an intriguing modern solution to the problem of restoring a historic monument. As it turns out, they are too heavy for the building and threaten to collapse. The repairs to the roof were not matched by any work on the interior, the ruined state of which has just been revealed to the public by the Benedictines who have reclaimed their monastery under new legislation. The future of Emmaus raises complex questions to do with the place of the Church in the new Czech and Slovak Republic, the need for adequate alternative facilities for those institutions invited to vacate their monastic headquarters, and the long-term problem of actually funding the considerable restoration programmes required.

Charles IV's town plan allowed for market squares of considerable dimensions. Charles Square – originally the cattle market – is the largest, measuring 530 by 150 metres. It was turned into a park in the nineteenth century, so has not been entirely surrendered to the modern traffic that makes itself felt much more in the New Town than elsewhere. No one building dominates the square, though the Jesuit

College and Church of St Ignatius (Kostel sv Ignáce) come close as they take up half of one side and, as in the Old Town, the statues on the façade, crowned by St Ignatius, carry the message of the Order to the outside world. At the top of the Square stands a reminder of an earlier age: the New Town Hall, the site of the first Defenestration of Prague. On 30 July 1419 the radical preacher Jan Želivský (d.1422) led a march to the Town Hall in protest against the failure to release some prisoners. The councillors deemed responsible were unceremoniously ejected, and the New Town established its credentials as a seat of radical Hussitism. There were often clashes with the Old Town as a result: after successfully fending off the 1420 crusade, the towns turned on each other, and Želivský himself was executed in the Old Town Square in 1422.

The Horse Market was the main axis of Charles IV's town and it has retained its central importance as Wenceslas Square. In the late eighteenth century the fortifications between the Old Town and the New were removed, thus turning the New Town towards the Old. Na příkopě (which means 'on the moat'), Wenceslas Square and Národní Street, the busy shopping and business districts of Prague, are known as the Golden Cross. There are a number of instructive ways of reading that cross, depending on whether one focuses on the huge stretch of Wenceslas Square, the triad of monuments to Czech nationalism at the extremities of the cross or the three segments as a whole.

Wenceslas Square is probably one of the best-known sights of Prague, having figured in many news reports of upheavals in the city, most recently in November 1989. On the 17th of that month, the official youth organisation, the SSM, was given permission to march on the anniversary of the murder of a Prague student by the Nazis; the demonstration moved from the cemetery towards Wenceslas Square where it was met by policemen with truncheons who wielded them with abandon. The events of that day set in motion a mass movement advocating reform, led by Civic Forum (Občanské Fórum), which brought together a number of opposition groups calling for the resignation of Communist leaders, investigation of police activities and the release of prisoners of conscience. Throughout the tumultuous events of that month, Wenceslas Square was packed with people. The 1912 equestrian statue of St Wenceslas was one focal point: the base was covered with candles, posters and photographs pleading for

Above There are a few buildings in Prague devoted to the city's strong musical heritage: in addition to the Museum of Music, there are museums dedicated to individual composers like Mozart, Smetana and Dvořák. The Dvořák Museum – shown here – is in the Michna Summer Palace which was built by Kilián Dientzenhofer in 1712–20. It has been restored recently and stands in graceful contrast to the university buildings around it on Ke Karlovu Street.

Below The Kilián Dientzenhofer Church of St John Nepomuk with its striking diagonally placed towers and curved façade has been poorly maintained.

change. The balcony of the Socialist Party's publishing house was made available to the activists and the square became a vast meeting hall addressed by a number of people including the dissident playwright, Václav Havel, and Alexander Dubček, leader of Czechoslovakia in 1968. They were soon to become President of the Republic and Chairman of the Federal Assembly.

Looking at the square, it is easy to fill it with crowds in one's mind's eye. The protesters of 1989 were standing in the same place as others who had taken issue with the ways in which they were ruled. On 21 August 1969 thousands marched to the square in protest on the anniversary of the Warsaw Pact invasion that had crushed the Prague Spring and Dubček's exploration of the possibilities of 'socialism with a human face'. Two deaths on Wenceslas Square had brought home the hopelessness of the situation: a child had been killed by Russian soldiers as he tried to push a Czech flag down the barrel of a tank, and on 16 January of that year, Jan Palach had set himself on fire.

Crowds had also gathered in the square when the Nazis invaded in 1938 and established the Protectorate of Bohemia and Moravia, as well as in 1918, to demonstrate in favour of independence. The proclamation of the Republic of Czechoslovakia was the – in a way unexpected – culmination of well over one hundred years of campaigning. The early National Revival was centred on the recovery of the Czech language and culture from underneath generations of Habsburg Germanization. In the European Spring of 1848 the citizens of Prague, like those of Paris, Vienna and other cities, took to the streets. On 12 June a crowd gathered in Wenceslas Square to celebrate mass on the occasion of the Pan-Slavonic Congress meeting in the city. There was clear tension between the Praguers and the imperial general, Prince Windischgratz. The ensuing riots were harshly put down, and hopes for reform extinguished.

While Vienna was consistently deaf to any campaigns for Bohemian autonomy and the political successes of the nineteenth century very limited, the National Revival succeeded in stimulating interest in Czech culture. It was a sign of the times when in 1786 actors from the new Nostitz Theatre gave performances in Czech in a wooden structure on Wenceslas Square. The experiment did not last long, but there are other, lasting monuments to that cultural awakening: the National Museum (Národní muzeum), the National Theatre (Národní divadlo) and the Municipal House.

The Vltava viewed from Vyšehrad.

The National Museum dominates Wenceslas Square, its imposing mass emphasized by the slight rise at the end of the square. It has the 'temple of culture' appearance familiar to museum-goers, but with the difference that the iconography of the building's decorative scheme is dedicated less to abstract ideals of enlightenment or classical virtues, than to Czechoslovakia. The idea of a museum came about as early as 1818 on the initiative of a group of aristocrats headed by Count Kaspar Sternberg, in whose palace the museum was originally housed. František Palacký organized the campaign to have a purpose-built home for the growing collection. The building, designed by Josef Schultz (1840–1917), was built between 1885 and 1891. The entrance hall, staircase and Pantheon are all decorated with statues, busts and history paintings paying tribute to the Czech nation that was coming into being.

Like the National Museum, the Municipal Museum (Muzeum hlavního města Prahy) is a product of the 1880s. Antonín Wiehl (1846–1910) and Antonín Balšánek (1865–1921) designed the building, which opened in 1898. The tympanum sculpture on the glory of history was destroyed in 1945 and replaced forty years later. Sadly, the Museum is now in a kind of no man's land by a railway bridge: it is rather ironic that the New Town should house a collection that successfully evokes the rich history of Prague. The prize of the collection is the Langweil model of Prague, with its miniature recreation of the Old Town, Lesser Quarter and most of Hradčany as they were in the early nineteenth century.

The same sense of cultural pride informs the National Theatre on Národní Street. There were crowds in attendance when the foundation stone was laid in 1868. Popular dedication to the cause was further proved when the new theatre built by Joseph Zítek (1832–1909) burned down shortly after it had opened; rebuilding started almost immediately, with funds raised by public subscription. Schultz was responsible for the second National Theatre, which opened on 18 November 1883 with a performance of Dvořák's Hussite Overture, which incorporates the two Hussite hymns, 'Ye Warriors of God' and 'The St Wenceslas Chorale'. The Theatre has been rebuilt and modernized recently, acquiring three new buildings in the process. The paintings and statues dedicated to theatrical and musical themes, including the history of Czech performance, were restored at the same time.

The architecture of the monumental and lavishly decorated National Museum and Theatre is described as Neo-Renaissance: one of the historical styles popular in late nineteenth-century Prague. The third building of national significance on the Golden Cross, the Municipal House, with its restaurants, meeting rooms and concert halls, was designed by Antonín Balsanek and Osvald Polívka (1859–1931) for the community of Prague between 1906 and 1912, when Art Nouveau – or Jugendstil – had come into vogue. Here too there is a strong emphasis on decorative effect, but there is also a clear interest in exploring the possibilities afforded by different materials and motifs – hence the use of mosaics, ceramic, stained glass and ironwork. One of the painters involved in the decoration of the House was Alfons Mucha (1860–1939). The Moravian artist, whose posters of Sarah Bernhardt popularized Art Nouveau in Paris, painted the allegories of civic virtues in the Hall of the Lord Mayor. Here too the political aspirations of Prague's Czech society were channelled along cultural lines. Starting with the mosaic on the façade, a Tribute to Prague, the different rooms all evoke local history and its heroes.

These buildings addressed the concerns of a specifically Czech nature: the German-speakers in Prague had no place in their contribution to a sense of cultural reawakening. Indeed, from the 1840s onwards there were aspects of the political demands of both sides that were in conflict. While both Czech- and German-speakers gathered at the meeting held at Wenceslas baths on 11 March 1848, the distinct demands of the former soon revealed the differing agendas of the two groups. The Czech vision of reform in Bohemia came to be bound up with a sense of Slav identity and Czech national society that precluded joint efforts at reform. Palacký refused an invitation to attend the 1848 Pan-German Congress in Frankfurt, stating that he was a Bohemian, of Slav race. He felt that the interests of his people would best be served by an Austrian federation.

By the time the buildings on the Golden Cross were commissioned, demography was on the side of Czech nationalism. In the 1830s and 1840s there was a majority of German-speakers in Prague; an 1846 census reported 66 046 Germans, 36 687 Czechs and 6 400 Jews. It was also the case that all of those in positions of authority in the army or the civil service were Germans, as were the higher clergy, the professional classes and the wealthy manufacturers and merchants. After 1850, land

Previous page Wenceslas Square, on the site of the New Town horse market, is the heart of modern Prague. More of a boulevard than a square, it measures 750 × 60 metres and is lined with nineteenth- and twentieth-century shops, office buildings, hotels and restaurants. The St Wenceslas Memorial of 1912 and the Neo-Renaissance National Museum in the upper part of the square are its best-known sights. Photograph: Julian Nieman, Susan Griggs Agency.

Above right The Neo-Renaissance building of the National Theatre burned down in 1881, shortly after it had opened and was rebuilt immediately. The best artists and sculptors were involved in decorating the building which reflected growing Czech national pride and aspirations.

Below right The Church of St Peter and St Paul dates back to the eleventh and twelfth centuries, when Vyšehrad was the seat of the Přemyslid princes. It underwent considerable rebuilding over the years: it was given its present Neo-Gothic appearance in 1885–1903.

reform and the industrialization of Bohemia meant that large numbers of peasants moved to the city: by 1900, German-speakers represented 6 per cent of a population of 500 000. The campaign for greater autonomy for Bohemia, originally launched by the intelligentsia, attracted the support of Czech-speaking citizens resentful of the limitations imposed by Vienna. While awaiting national results, they acquired power in Prague: from the 1860s they were in control of the city council.

The strong links that developed between Prague and Paris in the late nineteenth century were part of the Czech city's attempts to create non-Austrian ties. This was especially true after the creation in 1867 of the Austro-Hungarian Empire made it clear that the minorities under Habsburg rule were not going to be heard. The municipal council of Prague developed its own network of cultural exchanges: there were contacts between the city officials of Prague and Paris; the Sokol physical culture movement and French gymnasts; writers and artists. In 1902 Prague hosted a major Rodin exhibition, held in the Mánes Pavilion commissioned for that purpose; other exhibitions followed, and the opening up of cultural life in the city was of great importance to artistic circles in Prague.

All of these developments were countered by growing ethnic awareness among the German-speakers. The two groups led separate lives but there was tension in the streets, as the writer Milena Jesenká (1896–1944) recalled when discussing Sundays in Prague in the early part of this century: 'The Austrian students with their bright-coloured caps would stroll on the right side of the Prikiope and the Czechs in their Sunday best would promenade on the left side. Now and then a crowd would form, people would start singing something or other, and you could feel the exasperation in the air.'

The ethnic picture is of course further complicated by the presence of the Jews. While many of them were German-speakers, and some identified enough with German culture to volunteer at the outbreak of the First World War, there were also many who identified more with the Czechs. In 1900 there were 24 000 Jews in the Prague metropolitan area, of whom 14 145 stated that Czech was their language of daily use. Some of them emigrated to Israel after 1918, but most were at home in Masaryk's liberal republic. Czechs, Germans and Jews tended to go their separate ways in early twentieth-century Prague. This was

Above right A detail of the ironwork on the Art Nouveau Municipal House.

Below right The Art Nouveau entrance to At the Novaks on Vodickova Street.

Far right The Art Nouveau Grand Hotel Europa, situated in Wenceslas Square, was built in 1903–35.

The New Town has less of the immediate charm of the other royal towns of Prague but it has its share of intriguing façades.

reflected in the neighbourhoods of Prague: the Jews lived in and around Josefov, the former Jewish Town that was made a ward of Prague in 1852; the Germans in the New Town between Wenceslas Square and the Vltava, and many Czechs in the outskirts of the city. It was most unusual for them to mingle, as the avant-garde did at the Arco café in its heyday around 1912, and symptomatic, if extreme, that Milena Jesenká's father should have had her committed to an insane asylum for the folly of an affair with Ernest Polack, a Jew, whom she subsequently married.

It was against this background that the Czech majority set about providing Prague with its modern infrastructure. Zítek and Schultz, both professors at the Prague Technical College, influenced a whole generation of Prague architects. There was a heavy demand for their services as the city embarked on a considerable building programme to meet the demands of urbanization and local government. These architects are linked not with churches or palaces, but with office buildings, hotels, schools, banks, water and electricity plants, markets, restaurants, hospitals and villas. The late nineteenth-century buildings are often Neo-Renaissance in inspiration. Buildings like the former Zemská and Investment Banks at 18 and 20 Na příkopě with their allegorical mosaics in the lunettes under the cornice, the school on Vodičkova Street with its splendid red sgraffito façade, and Wiehl House on Wenceslas Square with its painted façade echo celebrated Prague buildings like Schwarzenberg Palace and At the Minute House (Dům U minuty).

Later buildings – contemporaneous with the Municipal House – move away from the historical style. On Národní Street, Polívka designed the Savings Bank (No 7) and the Topič publishing house (No 9), with their richly decorated façades. The grand gilded curves of the Hotel Europa on Wenceslas Square, and the turretted Koruna building gave an increasingly urban feel to the area that shortly before had still had the air of a provincial town, with its low Baroque houses. Jan Kotěra (1871–1923), the designer of the Mánes pavilion, used decorative stucco plant motifs on the façade of his Peterka House on the Square. Kotěra's later buildings reflect the gradual move away from decorative devices, historical or modern: he was an early advocate of a more functionalist approach to building, privileging purpose and materials over decoration.

The transition to a more functionalist approach to architecture in Prague involved an intriguing and short-lived phenomenon: Cubist architecture. In February 1911 the Group of Creative Artists was set up. Its members, inspired by the vision of painters like Picasso and Braque, explored the possibility of introducing those same sharp angles and sense of movement into three-dimensional forms. Many of their projects remained theoretical, but there are a few buildings in Prague with sharply modelled, prismatic façades which recast Baroque dynamism and interest in the play of light and shade in a modern idiom. The House of the Black Madonna (Dům U černé Matky Boží) by Josef Gočár (1880–1945) standing next to the Baroque houses on Celetná Street, and the Cubist niche for the statue next to Diamond House on Spalena Street, bring the two styles into close contact.

While architects Pavel Janák (1882–1956) and Gočár continued to experiment with these ideas in the early years of the new Republic – in the Rondo-cubist Legiobank on Na poříčí, or the Riunione Adriatica di Sicurtà – most buildings reflected a growing interest in functionalism. Just as the Prague architects had consistently attracted international attention with their contributions to Art Nouveau and Cubist architecture and design, the buildings of the 1920s and 1930s were at the vanguard of European architecture and recognized as such. On a visit in 1930, Le Corbusier felt that the modern buildings of Prague were the stuff of his dreams. The 1934 Pension Institute by Josef Havlíček (1899–1961) and Karel Honzik (1900–66) – now the Central Trade Union Council – as well as the 1930 Mánes Exhibition Hall still have the power to impress.

The 1920s and 1930s were the years of the first republic, when Prague, for so long the unofficial centre of a state coming into being, was a capital city in the fullest sense of the term. Government offices, embassies and other institutions had to be accommodated. These were also years of rapid population growth, largely the result of migration from rural areas and the influx of Germans and Jews from Germany and Austria, increasing the ethnic diversity that characterized the city until the Nazi occupation; after the war, the Czech government – along with those of Poland and Hungary – took the decision to expel those Germans remaining in the country. While the city acquired the trappings of the centre of government it also had to deal with urban problems of inadequate housing and public transportation. The

Charles IV, founder of the New Town, was responsible for much of the medieval building in Prague during the Golden Age when it was the capital of his Empire.

planners of the 1920s undertook to respect the architectural unity of the old towns of Prague; the city did not undergo the more thoroughgoing modernization of Vienna or Budapest.

The foresight of those planners, the work of conservationists as well as the vagaries of history ensured that the four royal towns of Prague are among the best preserved in Europe. The question now is how to preserve the past while providing for the future. This concerns not just Prague, but the country as a whole, which has more historic buildings per square kilometre than England. Many of them have been put to inappropriate use, others have been sadly neglected, still others over-restored. Concern has been expressed recently about the ability of the Czech institutions to cope singlehandedly with the enormous task of restoring and conserving this cultural heritage. This work will be done under entirely new circumstances: the new administration has political decisions to take concerning the fate of property confiscated in 1948 and establishing the powers of the local and national institutions responsible for historical monuments. The international circumstances have also changed, and there will now be opportunities for Western contribution to the preservation of these sites.

A recent 'Prague Resolution' along the lines of the Charter of Venice calls for the protection of the city's architectural heritage. There have been appeals for an end to injudicious development such as that marring the skyline of the New Town and the eastern suburbs, or the western hills above the Castle. Buildings that have hitherto been neglected, like the Art Nouveau apartment blocks, should also be restored. The material resources involved in the never-ending task of preserving such a wealth of historic buildings are of course immense, and the Resolution goes on to advocate international assistance to the relevant Czech institutions. This could involve everything from training to financial assistance and would fittingly involve a new set of people not just in the enjoyment but also in the preservation of what is – once again – the heart of Europe.

Travellers' Information

Travel and accommodation

There is no longer any mandatory currency exchange, nor is a visa required for British visitors. Czech currency may not be taken into or out of the country, but sterling, U.S. dollars and deutschmarks are easily exchanged in Prague. Deutschmarks, the most valued hard currency for ordinary Czechs, will probably command the best rates. Both Czechoslovak and British Airways make daily flights to Prague.

There is a wide and expanding range of hotels available as well as boatels on the Vltava, campsites and rooms to let. There are five categories of hotels, ranging from A* de luxe (****) to C(**).

The Alcron, 40 Štěpanska Street, Prague 1 (tel. 235 9296) and the Jalta, 45 Wenceslas Square, Prague 1 (tel. 26 55 41) are in the top category, as are the Ambassador, 5 Wenceslas Square (tel. 22 13 51/6) and The Three Ostriches (U tři pštrosů), 12 Druz ického Square, Prague 1 (tel. 53 61 51/5).

It is advisable to book well in advance as Prague is an increasingly popular – and crowded – destination. The London office of Cedok, the Czech travel bureau, can assist with hotel reservations or package tour bookings (17/18 Old Bond Street, London W1; tel. 071-629 6058).

In Prague, Cedok, 5 Panska Street, Prague 1 (tel. 22 56 57) and Pragotour, U Obecniho domu 23 Prague 1 can also assist with accommodation.

Good restaurants are still few and far between in Prague; the best two in the city are at present the tiny and intimate Opera Grill and At The Three Ostriches – both need to be booked well in advance.

Public transport in the city includes buses, trams and the Metro. Generally speaking, historic Prague can easily be visited on foot, or seen from boat trips along the river Vltava.

Tourist services

Pragotour will arrange guided tours. The Cedok office at 18 Na příkopě, Prague 1 (tel. 212 71 11) provides a wide range of services for visitors, as does the Prague Information Service, 20 Na příkopě, Prague 1. While English is spoken, many more people understand German.

In planning a visit to Prague it should be borne in mind that the city is necessarily in a state of flux given the tremendous changes that are taking place after the revolution. Opening times may be altered, restaurants may have changed hands and advertised prices risen. Conversely, some things may not have changed: it may still prove difficult to visit some churches as their opening times are unfathomable and some sites, like the Týn Court or the Smetana Museum, may well be closed to the public because they are still – after a number of years – under restoration.

Art museums

The National Gallery Collection is open 1000–1800 and closed on Monday. It is divided between:

The Sternberg Palace, 15 Hradčany Square, Prague 1 (nineteenth- and twentieth-century European art);

St George's Convent in the Castle (Early Bohemian art);

Goltz-Kinský Palace, 12 Old Town Square (graphic art);

St Agnes Convent, 17 U milosrdnych (nineteenth-century Czech art).

The most interesting works from the National Gallery Collection are those housed in St George's Convent, which include very fine thirteenth- and fourteenth-century altarpieces and wooden sculptures.

The Loreta convent in Hradčany houses Prague's treasury, which contains a collection of magnificent Baroque monstrances. The Strahov Monastery, also in Hradčany, is Prague's Museum of National Literature, and the site of the well-preserved Theological Hall (1671–9) and Philosophical Hall (1782–4) libraries.

History museums

The Museum of the City of Prague, Nové sady J Švermy, Prague 8, is open 0900–1200; 1300–1700 except on Monday.

The National Museum, 68 Wenceslas Square, Prague 1 is open 0900–1700 except on Tuesday.

The State Jewish Museum exhibitions in the synagogues

of Josefov, Prague 1 are open 0900–1700 except on Saturday.

The exhibition at Lobkowic Palace in the Castle is open 0830–1700 except on Monday.

The Military Museum, Schwarzenberg Palace, Hradčany Square is open May to October, 0900—1530 Monday to Friday and 0900–1700 on Saturday and Sunday.

The Smetana Museum, 1 Novotněho lavka, Prague 1 is open 1000–1700 except on Tuesday.

The Dvořák Museum, 20 Ke Karlovu, Prague 2, is open 1000–1700 except on Tuesday.

The Bertramka Mozart Museum, 169 Mozartova, Prague 5, is open 1000–1700 except on Tuesday.

Cultural events

Monthly guides to what is on in Prague provide information on concerts, plays and temporary exhibitions. During the spring months many and varied concerts in concert halls, churches and convents are organized by the Prague Spring Music Festival, offering an unparalleled range of Czech and international music. A number of excellent mime companies give regular performances at theatres throughout the city.

Other places of interest

Near Prague these include Charles IV's Karlštejn Castle; White Mountain and the Star Summer Palace (Palac Hvězda), a Renaissance hunting lodge; Troja Palace, built by Jean-Baptiste Mathey in 1679–85 and Břevnov Monastery, rebuilt by Kilían Dientzenhofer in 1700–20. Those wishing to travel further afield have a wealth of monasteries, castles, cities, towns and landscapes to discover in Bohemia, Moravia and Slovakia.

Further reading

Art and architecture

Blazicek, Oldrich Jan, *Baroque Art in Bohemia*, London, 1979

Cannon-Brookes, P. and C., *Baroque Churches*, London, 1978

Horejsi, Jirina, *Renaissance Art in Bohemia*, London, 1979

Knox, Brian, *Bohemia and Moravia: an Architectural Companion*, London, 1962

Kutal, Albert, *Gothic Art in Bohemia and Moravia*, London, 1971

History and biography

Brook, Stephen, *The Double Eagle: Vienna, Budapest, Prague*, London, 1988

Buber-Neumann, Margarete, *Mílena*, London, 1989

Havel, Vaclav, *Disturbing the Peace*, London, 1990

Pawel, Ernest, *The Nightmare of Reason: A Life of Franz Kafka*, London, 1988

Index